# Gold Medal 'Misfits'
## How the unwanted Canadian hockey team
## scored Olympic glory

D0872536

# Pat MacADAM

Manor House Publishing

**Library and Archives Canada
Cataloguing in Publication**

MacAdam, Pat
    Gold medal "misfits" : how the unwanted 1948
Flyers scored Olympic glory / Pat MacAdam.

Includes index.
ISBN 978-0-9781070-6-2

    1. RCAF Flyers (Hockey team)--History.
2. Hockey players--Canada--Interviews.
3. Olympic Winter Games (5th : 1948 : Saint
Moritz, Switzerland)
I. Title.

GV848.4.C3M32 2007          796.962'66
    C2007-905318-1

Cover photo, interior photos used with permission
Back cover author photo courtesy The Ottawa Sun

Published by Manor House Publishing Inc.
4522 Cottingham Crescent, Ancaster, Ontario,
Canada, L9G 3V6
905-648-2193… Fax: 905-648-8369
www.manor-house.biz

We acknowledge the financial support of the
Government of Canada through the Book
Publishing Industry Development Program (BPIDP)
for our publishing activities.

Dedicated to she who must be obeyed - my patient wife and best friend, Janet, with apologies for the many hours she spent looking at my back while I worked at the keyboard.

TABLE OF CONTENTS

# A Word from the Publisher

**Pat MacAdam** has made a major contribution to hockey history with his skilful telling of the truly unbelievable saga of a rag tag group of talented amateur hockey players who met and surmounted incredible odds to win the World's and Olympic championships in St. Moritz, Switzerland, in 1948.

After concluding Canada could not ice a team whose players could honestly sign the Olympic Oath they were amateurs, the Canadian government announced it would not send a team to the 1948 Olympics.

The Royal Canadian Air Force assembled a team but it was viewed with skepticism by government and public. The team tried proving itself in an exhibition game against a university team and was trounced. Their modicum of public support then vanished.

The team scrounged equipment and slept in fleabag hotels. The day before departure from Ottawa, their regular goaltender failed his RCAF medical. His replacement met the team, for the first time, on the train to New York. The behind-scenes story is recounted in fascinating detail by MacAdam in his unique story-telling style, based on interviews with all of the living Flyers and other key players.

At the Olympics, the team won seven games and tied one. Their goaltender had five shutouts and allowed only five goals in the eight games: An incredible achievement that has never received its recognition – until now. This is a remarkable must-read tale of adversity, triumph and redemption.

- *Michael B. Davie,* author, *Winning Ways*

# Reviews and Endorsements

*"...the Cinderella story of one of Canada's most successful and least known hockey teams that won Gold at the 1948 Olympics in St. Moritz. This highly readable volume pieces together the incredible odyssey of this amazing group of amateurs, from their original try-out camp to their triumphant homecoming.*

*It should be read as a great sports saga but it is equally fascinating as a tale of human achievement against impossible odds.*

*Pat MacAdam combines the warm skills of a born storyteller with the cold eye of a stubborn investigative reporter and works his beat hard. The results make for an impressive story, well told."*
**Peter C Newman**, author *The Canadian Establishment*

*"... the best storyteller I have ever encountered and I have met and read the best."*
**Mordecai Richler**, author, *Barney's Version*

*"...outstanding... nostalgic...Canadian treasure,"*
**Brian McFarlane**, Hockey Night In Canada

"...a tale of determination, grit and colorful personalities. MacAdam's painstaking research strings together the story of a perceived under-dog team's bold quest for world hockey Gold. As a rabid fan, I saw many of the Flyers playing for various teams in Eastern Canada. I believe a half-dozen of them would be stars in today's NHL.
**Doug Fisher**, columnist, former Chair, Hockey Canada

## MacAdam scores hat trick with new book

Canadians love come-from-behind stories about underdogs who persevere against incredible odds. That being said, readers of Pat MacAdam's **Gold Medal 'Misfits'** are in for a real treat.

It's a highly enjoyable account of what most people at the time considered to be a rag-tag bunch of second-rate hockey players who served in the RCAF in the Second World War. The squad was selected to represent Canada in St. Moritz, Switzerland, at the 1948 Winter Olympics.

To say they were unlikely candidates for the gold medal would be an understatement. Another Canadian who brought home Olympic Gold, Barbara Ann Scott (King), writes in a foreword to the book that the team's beginnings were a disaster. The world-renowned figure skater says that press and fans alike thought the team should stay home.

"I remember skating between periods of an exhibition game in Ottawa and our Flyers were shut out 7-0 by McGill University," says Canada's sweetheart of the 1948 Olympics, noting RCAF squadron leader Sandy Watson refused to admit defeat and knew the team could achieve gold medal glory.

MacAdam's laid-back yet insightful writing style will transport the reader back 60 years to the heady days when a hockey miracle brought the gold home to Canada.

- **Tom Douglas**, author of six books, including three bestsellers on World War II and **Permission Granted**, memoirs of an RCAF Squadron Leader

# Gold Medal 'Misfits'
How the unwanted Canadian hockey team
scored Olympic glory

# Pat MacADAM

Manor House Publishing

## Other bestsellers by the same author:

***Our Century in Sport*** (Fitzhenry and Whiteside, 2002, ISBN 1-55041-636-7)

***Big Cy and other Characters:*** *Pat MacAdam's Cape Breton* (Biography, Cape Breton University Press, 2005 ISBN 1-897009-12-7)

***Unbelievable Canadian War Stories****: Well Beyond the Call of Duty* (Altitude Publishing, 2006, ISBN 1554390516)

# About the Author

**Pat MacAdam** is a highly respected popular columnist/journalist with the Ottawa Sun and Sun Media Group whose feature writing work has been short-listed for National Newspaper Awards.

He's also the author of several national bestsellers, including *Our Century in Sport; Big Cy and other Characters: Pat MacAdam's Cape Breton;* and, *Unbelievable Canadian War Stories: Well Beyond the Call of Duty.*

A prolific freelance writer, his work has also appeared in The National Post; Cape Breton Post; Saint John Telegraph Journal, Vancouver Sun, Macleans Magazine; Sun Media, The Beaver, Canadian Magazine and other major publications.

Prior to achieving national prominence as a columnist/journalist and author, MacAdam spent 40 years in Tory backroom politics, serving leaders from John Diefenbaker to Brian Mulroney. His memoirs of these years are to be featured in an upcoming biographical book to be published by Manor House Publishing in the fall of 2008.

MacAdam was senior consultant and director of Government Consultants International and is the former Minister Counsellor-Press and Media (Press Officer) for the Canadian High Commission, at Trafalgar Square, London.

From 1979-87 he served as Senior Advisor to Brian Mulroney, during Mulroney's years as President, Iron Ore Co. of Canada, Leader of the Opposition and Prime Minister of Canada.

Prior to this he was a speech writer to other political leaders and was a successful businessman.

He resides in Ottawa with his wife Janet.

Manor House Publishing
www.manor-house.biz  905-648-2193

# Foreword
By Barbara Ann Scott King

This is the story of a real life miracle I was privileged to witness.

There is no fiction involved. It is truthful and magnificently told by the renowned writer and author, Pat MacAdam.

The year was 1948 and I remember it as if it were yesterday.

We were a small band of Canadian athletes chosen to represent Canada in the first Olympic Games since 1936. The Canadian Amateur Hockey Association couldn't find a hockey team "amateur" enough to represent Canada. But, Dr. "Sandy" Watson, then a Squadron Leader/Medical Officer in the Royal Canadian Air Force, knew there were gifted hockey players in the RCAF who could qualify as "amateurs," could form a team and win a Gold Medal.

It was his courage and determination that made it possible and made it happen, as Pat MacAdam reconstructs in his painstakingly researched account.

Pat MacAdam's book of the 1948 RCAF Flyers ranks as one of hockey's greatest reconstructions – a veritable detective story – a jig saw puzzle put together painstakingly almost 60 years later.

The team's beginnings were rather a disaster. I remember skating between periods of an exhibition game in Ottawa and our Flyers were shut out 7-0 by McGill University.

The press and fans alike said the Flyers should stay home. Dr. "Sandy" hung in there, added more players and, when they arrived in Europe, they soared to Olympic Gold with seven wins and a tie in the eight game championships.

I am so proud to have been on the same Canadian Olympic team as the Flyers and, to this day, many of us are still in touch.

Pat MacAdam relates a truly stirring and inspiring story that makes us all proud to be Canadians.

**Barbara Ann Scott King**
Amelia Island, Florida

# Introduction
## By 'Sandy' Watson

No writer is better qualified to tell the 1948 RCAF Flyers story than Pat MacAdam.

He is a self-confessed Flyers' "junkie" and has followed our achievements and our after-lives with "awe and admiration."

If I may indulge in some modest self-praise, there is much to be in awe of and there is much to admire. A group of talented hockey players was thrown together at the last minute and went on to win the Olympic and World hockey championships in St. Moritz, Switzerland.

When I saw the Ottawa Journal head: CANADA WILL NOT BE REPRESENTED IN OLYMPIC HOCKEY AT ST. MORITZ IN 1948, my reaction, after I peeled myself off the ceiling, was: "We can't get a hockey team? NUTS TO THAT!"

When I say "last minute" I mean last minute. One of the players met the team for the first time on the train to New York to board an ocean liner to Southampton. He had never seen the Flyers play and they had never seen him play before until our first exhibition game in London.

The RCAF Flyers showed the world the embodiment of the human spirit and the true meaning of teamwork. The players bonded on the ocean voyage and somewhere between Ottawa and St. Moritz they jelled as a team.

They played as a team and, while there were some players more gifted than others, in the end it was teamwork that won them Olympic Gold.

Since 1948, the young men who came together as a team have stayed together as a family and we have kept in close touch over the years and across the provinces.

Pat MacAdam has written major articles on us for the Ottawa Citizen, the Toronto and Ottawa Suns and for military magazines. He has been present at major functions when we were honoured by the Canadian forces as their athletes of the century.

We invited Pat MacAdam to be a member of our diminishing family. At a luncheon in the Rideau Club in Ottawa we named him the only living "Honorary RCAF Flyer" and presented him with the last remaining Flyers' enamelled lapel pin from 1948.

Pat and I have spent hours on the 'phone and he has visited me in my home. We sit in my sunroom together with his tape recorder. Pat has interviewed every living Flyer and every time we speak he astounds me. I thought I knew everything there was to know about the Flyers but he always manages to come up with something I didn't know.

**A. Gardner Watson**, O.C. C.M., M.D., F.A.C.S., F.R.C.S.(C)
("Sandy" Watson passed away in December, 2003)

## FORGOTTEN HEROES

This is a story about heroes a nation has forgotten – the 1948 RCAF Flyers' hockey team.

They barnstormed through Europe for 2 ½ months on a wing and a prayer. They sang for their suppers, relying on gate receipts in 34 exhibition games for expense money.

Some men are born great; some had greatness thrust upon them and others, like the RCAF Flyers, reached down and pulled greatness up to their level.

In January, 1948, when they left Ottawa for the Olympics in St. Moritz, Switzerland, they were written off by Canadians. A month later, they were being lionized around the world as Olympic and World hockey champions.

Somewhere between Ottawa's Union Station and St. Moritz, a rag-tag collection of last minute selections came together and became the toast of the world.

Many of the players were retracing routes they took when they fought a war that paralyzed all of Europe. This trip, they would not have to endure cramped frigid bombers, probing enemy searchlights, red hot shrapnel from German antiaircraft guns or the frightening experience of jumping out of a doomed aircraft over enemy held territory.

When they boarded the liner, Queen Elizabeth, for their first Atlantic crossing, they carried kitbags and rifles. Their second crossing was more tranquil. They were going to Europe with hockey sticks to reclaim the world hockey supremacy Canada lost to Great Britain in the 1936 Olympics in Garmisch-Partenkirchen, Germany.

The Flyers were 17 determined young men who did not have the word "defeat" in their vocabularies. From the beginning, they considered themselves the team that could and they did.

Hubie Brooks was going back wearing the ribbons of the Military Cross and two of Poland's highest decorations for gallantry. He was the Navigator/Bomb Aimer on a Wellington bomber assigned to attack Hamburg, one of the most heavily defended cities in Germany. His plane was shot down. He was badly injured when he bailed out. The rest of his war was waged on the ground. He was taken prisoner, escaped three times, was re-captured twice and fought the rest of his war in the hills with Polish guerilla fighters.

Bomb Aimer Roy Forbes was luckier than Hubie Brooks. When his Lancaster bomber was shot down in northwest Europe, he bailed out and managed to avoid capture. He was on the loose for almost five months while being passed along the French-Belgian Underground escape network.

Frank Dunster saw his Europe through the bombsight of a Halifax bomber during 200 hours in the air on 37 bombing raids over Berlin, Essen and Cologne – one complete tour of duty plus seven missions. He was returning, wearing the distinctive ribbon of the Distinguished Flying Cross on his tunic.

The Flyers traveled and played under the most appalling conditions – on outdoor natural ice surfaces in rainstorms and snowstorms, on rinks covered with water and slush and in thin altitudes more than a mile above sea level.

The Flyers had not played competitive games outdoors since they were kids playing shinny on ponds and rivers. As adults they played on artificial ice at Maple Leaf Gardens, Montreal Forum, the Ottawa Auditorium and the Hull Arena.

The team traveled 15,000 miles through eight countries. They endured transportation in steerage, sub-standard meals and accommodation in an area of the world still recovering from the ravages of a World War and subsistence level food rationing.

They dressed for games at their hotels and took buses to the rinks. There were no dressing rooms or showers at any of the rinks. In St. Moritz, their trainer, George McFaul, made 60-mile round trips by train to have their skates sharpened. They carried their own gear in RCAF kitbags slung over their shoulders.

Their pay was basic RCAF allowances that would be looked upon today as well below the minimum wage. To a man, they told me they would have "played for nothing" – for the honor and glory of representing their country at the Olympic Games.

A team not accorded a "hope in Hell of winning" played 42 games against the best of the rest of the world. They won 31 games, lost five and tied six. The only national team to beat them was Switzerland's in a pre-Olympic exhibition warm-up game 6,000 feet up in the Swiss Alps.

Obviously, Canada's 2006 Olympic hockey team was ignorant of Santayana's admonition that if you do not learn from history you are doomed to repeat it.

"Sandy" Watson and Frank Boucher managed and coached military hockey teams in Europe in the post-war era. They were familiar with many European teams and their networks of expatriate Canadians playing in Europe provided up-to-date scouting reports.

Canada's 2006 Olympians hit the ice in Europe cold turkey. They had never played before as a team. They had never faced European competition on larger ice surfaces. They failed to take into consideration that many of the European teams were club teams that played together for years and were strengthened by nationals playing in the National Hockey League.

The 1948 RCAF Flyers left Ottawa for Europe weeks before the Winter Games opened in St. Moritz.

The team played exhibition games in the London area against strong British teams composed mainly of Canadians. Next, they flew to Paris and played an exhibition game against Le Club de Racing de Paris – the strongest professional senior team in all of Europe. Le Club de Racing was a team composed of Canadians, many of whom went on to star in the Quebec Senior League.

The Flyers built up an early 3-0 lead but travel fatigue and two bonehead defensive giveaways cost them the win. The Paris team won 5-3.

As a medical doctor, "Sandy" Watson was well aware of the fall-out from hypoxia – known commonly as mountain sickness – the effects of high altitudes on those unacclimated to it.
Hypoxia can diminish blood oxygenation and result in mental confusion.

Consequently, the Flyers played pre-Olympics' exhibition games against strong Swiss teams in Davos, Basel, Arosa and St. Moritz. Some of these towns are the highest altitude (6,000 feet +) resort towns in all of Europe.

The Flyers adjusted well to the thinner air and none of the players suffered any side effects.

In 1960, the Gold Medal United States squad trained wisely for their seven games Olympic schedule.

Before leaving for Squaw Valley, California, the American team played 18 exhibition games – won 10, lost four and tied four.

The U.S. team swept their seven games with a perfect 7-0-0 record. They defeated a rag tag Canadian team 2-1 and the USSR 3-2 – the first time the U.S. had beaten Russia in world and Olympic ice hockey.

The Flyers came home to glory in April. Sportswriters who once looked down on them as bums saluted them as gods. They called them "The Captains of the Clouds" and then promptly forgot them.

Half the team is dead now. The other half is in the twilight of life.

## CANADA'S PERSONAL SANDBOX

Canada dominated world hockey competition from the time the first puck was dropped in Antwerp in 1920 until the 1936 Games in Garmisch-Partenkirchen, Germany. Canadian teams won 16 consecutive games and four consecutive Olympic titles.

They scored 209 goals and gave up only eight. Canadian goaltenders recorded 12 shutouts in 16 games.

Along the road to glory, Canada administered some awesome thrashings – 15-0 and 30-0 over Czechoslovakia, 22-0, 11-0 and 20-0 over Sweden, 33-0 and 13-0 over Switzerland, 19-2 and 14-0 over Great Britain and 22-0 over France.
In a 33-0 win over Switzerland, Canada led 18-0 at the end of the first period.

None of the lopsided scores comes even close to a thrashing Canada laid on Denmark in a non-Olympic year. In 1949, Sudbury Wolves obliterated Denmark 47-0 but Czechoslovakia defeated Canada, for the first time ever, by a score of 3-2 to win the World title.

Canada's monopoly on world hockey supremacy ended at the 1936 Olympic Games in Garmisch-Partenkirchen, Germany. A team from Great Britain, stacked with 10 Canadian players, upset reigning Allan Cup champions, Port Arthur Bearcats, 2-1 to win Gold.

Then, with the outbreak of World War 11, the lights went out around the world. The Olympic flame was doused and would not be re-lit until 1948 in St. Moritz.

The RCAF Flyers reclaimed Gold for Canada in 1948 and, four years later in Oslo, Norway, Edmonton Mercurys won seven games and tied the United States 3-3 for the Gold Medal position on the victory dais.

It would be 50 years later - to the day – the 2002 Olympic Games in Salt Lake City – before another Canadian team composed of All-Star National Hockey League players stood on a podium to have Olympic Gold medals hung around their necks.

Between 1920 and 1952 – seven sets of Olympic Games – teams from Canada won 37 games, tied three and lost only one. They scored 403 goals and allowed only 34.

## 1920 IN ANTWERP

Hockey and figure skating first cracked the lineup of Olympic sports at the Summer Games in Antwerp, Belgium, in 1920. Hockey was a sport that Games organizers accepted reluctantly.

Hockey was not wanted on the voyage until the operators of Le Palais de Glace stadium refused the use of the facility for figure skating unless hockey was also included.

Theresa Wald of the U.S.A., a Bronze Medalist, included a Salchow in her figure skating programme and was reprimanded by judges for "unfeminine behaviour" and threatened she would be penalized.

Even then, canny rink owners knew there were big bucks in the exciting, fast moving and violent spectator sport.

Figure skating and hockey were allowed in as "demonstration" sports. It was not until 1983, 63 years later, that the International Olympic Committee stamped "official" on the 1920 results.

From 1920 on, the team that won Olympic Gold was also crowned World champion. Five European nations – Belgium, France, Switzerland, Czechoslovakia and Sweden – and Canada and the United States competed. Germany and Austria were not welcome. The memories of World War One were still too painful.

Significant rule changes were introduced at Antwerp. The seventh man – the "rover" – was dropped.

There would be no changing "on the fly".

Teams played two 20-minute halves separated by a 10-minute intermission.

Highly respected W.A. Hewitt, Foster's father, was Secretary of the Canadian team and refereed the very first game in Olympic history – a contest between Belgium and Sweden.

The Swedes dressed like soccer players. They did not wear shoulder, elbow or shin pads. W.A. Hewitt said their goaltender wore what looked like "a cross between a blacksmith's apron and an aviator's coat".

Europeans were bowled over by the Canadians' aggressive style of play. A by-lined article by Oscar Soderlund in Stockholm-Tidninger reported:

*"Every single player on the rink (Canada-USA game) was a perfect acrobat on skates, skated at tremendous speed without regard to himself or*

*anyone else, jumped over sticks and players with ease and grace, turned sharply with perfect ease and without losing speed, and skated backwards just as easily as forward. And, during all this, the puck was held down on the ice and was dribbled forward by means of short shoves of the stick."*

The United States' team had seven Canadian born players.

International Ice Hockey Federation President, Max Sillig, played for the Swiss team – the only IOC president ever to participate in Olympic Games while holding office.

Switzerland was thumped 29-0 by the Americans who scored twice while playing two men shorthanded.

The Americans "winked" at the amateur status rule for Olympians. Jerry "Duke" Geran, from Holyoke, Mass., played college hockey for Dartmouth but in 1917-18 he played four games with Montreal Wanderers of the National Hockey League.

In 1921-22, he played eight games for the professional Paris, France, Volants.

In 1925-26 he played 33 games with Boston Bruins and managed four goals and one assist. Czechoslovakia lost 16-0 to the United States and 15-0 to Canada. Canada defeated Sweden 12-1 and the U.S. 2-0.

Through the luck of the draw, Czechoslovakia defeated Sweden 1-0 to win a Bronze medal despite being outscored 31-1 in their three games.

Canada was represented by the Winnipeg Falcons who had just won the Allan Cup by defeating University of Toronto.

## THE WINNIPEG FALCONS

The Falcons were the pariahs of senior hockey in Winnipeg. Every Falcon, except substitute, Alan "Huck" Woodman, was of Icelandic descent.

Establishment Winnipeg looked down on the second-generation Icelandic immigrants as rabble and dregs of society and refused to admit their team in the city senior league.

So, hockey players of Icelandic birth formed their own league and, in the end, they had the last laugh.

The senior Falcons won the Allan Cup in 1920. They defeated University of Toronto 8-3 and 3-2 in the final series. The following year the junior Falcons, formed from the Young Men's Lutheran Club of the Icelandic Lutheran Church of Canada, won the Memorial Cup in Toronto's Arena Gardens.

The junior Falcons sailed past Regina Vics and then crushed Fort William YMCA 9-3 and 11-4 to win the western Canada championship. They met Stratford in the Memorial Cup final and won the opening game of the two-games, total goals series 9-2. The Cup very nearly slipped from their lips when Howie Morenz scored a hat trick to pace Stratford to a 7-2 win. But, the Falcons prevailed and won the series eleven goals to nine.

The Allan Cup champion Falcons were still in Toronto when they received word they would be going to Antwerp to represent Canada. There wasn't enough time for the team to return to Winnipeg so the hat was passed to buy the players new clothes for overseas. Each player was given a $25 clothing allowance. The team sailed from Saint John, New Brunswick, on the CPR liner "MELITA".

The Falcons purchased cured wood in Montreal and the ship's carpenter fashioned two dozen sticks for the team to use in Europe.

The team arrived in Antwerp April 14 and was given a rousing welcome by British troops stationed in Belgium and by the Belgians. Six members of the Falcons' team fought in France and Belgium during World War One.

Frank Frederickson was the big gun for the Falcons in Antwerp. In the 1920 Allan Cup playoffs he scored 22 goals in six games. At the Olympics, he scored 12 goals in three games.

Teammate Haldor "Slim" Halderson scored nine times. Both went on to modest careers in the National Hockey League.

Frederickson's career was more enduring. He played 161 NHL games with Boston, Detroit, Pittsburgh, Detroit and Victoria and scored 39 goals. He also played in three Stanley Cup finals and won cups with Victoria and Boston.

Halderson played in just 44 NHL games. He was a much traveled journeyman with stops in Detroit, Toronto, Saskatoon, Victoria, Quebec, Newark, Kansas City, Duluth, Tulsa and Wichita. He played on one Stanley Cup winner with Victoria.

Another Falcon, Robert Benson, played eight games with Boston Bruins in 1924-25 and his minor league career took him to Winnipeg, Calgary, Edmonton, Moose Jaw, Minneapolis, Seattle and Hollywood.

In March, 1920, a Falcon player won the North American speed skating championship.

The Falcons played one game too many. On their way back home, they played an exhibition game against Ottawa in the Auditorium before 6,000 fans. Ottawa were 20-1 underdogs but they thumped the Falcons 4-1.

Both teams were guests at a Chateau Laurier luncheon.

The Icelandic team that Wasp Winnipeg looked down on as pariahs and outcasts came home to Winnipeg – Olympic and World hockey champions. On May 22, 1920, thousands turned out to salute them in a huge downtown parade. That night, they rubbed shoulders with 400 of Winnipeg's elite at a glittering banquet in the Fort Garry Hotel.

What a difference a Gold Olympic Medal makes!

## 1924 IN CHAMONIX

The first "Official" Olympic Winter Games were staged in Chamonix in 1924. The Games were called "International Winter Sports Week".

Canada was represented by Toronto Granites, a team composed largely of ex-servicemen. Granites won the Allan Cup by defeating Regina Victorias 6-2 and 7-0 in Toronto.

The Toronto Star chose not to cover the Games. So, they contracted with one of the players, Harry Watson (not NHLer Harry Watson), to send a series of breezy freelance articles back to Toronto. In one article he wrote that the team had an especially rough ocean crossing, which moved one player to remark: "Why the ---don't they hold the Games in Oakville?"

Toronto Granites took the Gold Medal by storm. They set a scoring record that may never be matched. They scored 110 goals in five games and allowed only three.

Granites defeated Switzerland 33-0, Czechoslovakia 30-0, Sweden 29-0, Great Britain 19-2 and the United States 6-1.

Left winger Harry Watson from St. John's, Newfoundland, was a one man wrecking crew. He scored 37 goals – six goals in one period in a game against Czechoslovakia - and 13 goals against Switzerland. Bert McCaffrey scored 20 goals, "Hooley" Smith 18, Dunc Munro 16 and Beattie Ramsay 10.

Harry Watson potted 13 goals in five games in Allan Cup playoffs.

Chamonix was Watson's finest hour. In a rough final game against the U.S., he was knocked out cold two minutes after the opening faceoff. The trainer revived him and he went back out and scored the first two goals of the game.

Watson never did regain his scoring touch after the Olympics and spent the rest of his career playing senior hockey in mercantile leagues around Toronto.

Dunc Munro, Bert McCaffrey and "Hooley" Smith went on to play in the NHL. Smith played on Stanley Cup winners with Ottawa Senators and Montreal Maroons and Munro and McCaffrey won Cups with Montreal Maroons.

"Hooley" Smith scored 211 goals and added 223 assists in 769 games with Ottawa Senators, Montreal Maroons, Boston Bruins and New York Americans. He played on Allan Cup winners in

1922 and 1923 and Stanley Cup winners in 1927 and 1935.

"Hooley" Smith was named to the NHL First All-Star team in 1936 and the second All-Star team in 1932. He was elected to the Hockey Hall of Fame in 1972.

"Taffy" Abel, a Chippewa Indian from Sault Ste Marie, Michigan, was the captain of the U.S. squad. He scored 15 goals. He went on to play eight seasons in the NHL with New York Rangers and Chicago Black Hawks.

## ST. MORITZ in 1928

Winning Olympic Gold was becoming routine for Canada. All they had to do was show up. Olympic organizers realized that other nations were not in the same league as Canada. So, Canada was given an automatic bye into the final round.

Another Toronto team, Allan Cup champion Toronto Graduates, the 1926 University of Toronto squad that had stayed together, represented Canada. The United States did not send a team to St. Moritz.

The Grads almost didn't make it. Fort William gave them a run for their money in the Allan Cup finals played in Vancouver. The teams tied the opening game 2-2 and Fort William squeezed out a 3-2 overtime win in the second game. Grads took the third game 4-1 and edged past Fort William 2-1 in overtime in the fourth game.

The coach of the Toronto Grads was Constantine Falkland Kerrys Smythe, better known as Conn.

Twenty-five nations competed in the Games. The Opening Ceremonies were held in a blinding snowstorm and below freezing temperatures. There were only 300 spectators in the stands.

Canada won the hockey competition in a cakewalk. The Grads blasted past Sweden, Great Britain and Switzerland – all by double digit shutouts. Canada outscored the opposition 38-0. All games were played outdoors on natural ice. Four days after the frigid opening the weather turned warmer and the rinks were reduced to slush. Officials marked deeper puddles with orange peels to warn skaters.

Unseasonably warm weather forced cancellation of one speed skating event and the bobsled competition was cut back from four runs to two. Fortunately, four days later a cold front moved back in.

Canada's goaltender was Joe Sullivan who later became one of Canada's leading eye, ear, nose and throat specialists. He was also knighted by the Pope. In 1957, he was in the first intake of Progressive Conservative Senators appointed by then Prime Minister John Diefenbaker.

Obviously, he didn't have much work in the nets while racking up two shutouts. During one game, when his teammates had built up a healthy lead, he skated over to the boards and signed autographs while play went on. "Stuffy" Mueller tended nets in the third game and shut out Great Britain 14-0.

Olympic rules in 1928 did not permit a goaltender to drop to his knees and defencemen were not allowed to play the puck with their skates in their own end.

Senator Sullivan's brother, Frank, was also a member of the Gold Medal Canadian team and both had sons who played pro hockey.

Joe's son, Frank, won an Allan Cup with Toronto Marlboros and played a handful of games with Toronto Maple Leafs and Chicago Black Hawks. He also played eight seasons in the American Hockey League with Pittsburgh, Buffalo and Springfield.

Frank's son, Peter, played two NHL seasons with Winnipeg and scored 28 goals. He spent six seasons playing in Switzerland and averaged 40 goals a year with Langnau.

## LAKE PLACID, 1932

The world was still in the trough of a global Depression. Only four countries entered teams in the 1932 Lake Placid Olympics hockey tournament – defending Gold medallist Canada, Germany, United States and Poland.

Sweden, 1928 Silver medalists, and Switzerland, Bronze medal winners, did not send teams.

Before 1932, the only Medals won by Canadian athletes were for hockey.

At Lake Placid, Canadian speed skaters Alexander Hurd, William Logan, Frank Stack and Montgomery Wilson won one Silver and five Bronze medals.

Only 17 nations and 306 athletes participated in the Lake Placid Games, compared with 495 in St Moritz in 1928 and 755 in Germany in 1936.

The Lake Placid Games were the first held outside Europe and many nations gave travel, time and expense as their reasons for not participating.

The Games were not only savaged by the Depression. Mild weather in mid-February forced organizers to truck snow in from Canada.

Franklin D. Roosevelt was Governor of New York and formally opened the Games. His First Lady, Eleanor, tried out the bobsled run.

Sonja Henie successfully defended her figure skating title.

American Rhodes Scholar Eddie Eagan recorded an Olympic first that has never been equalled. He is the only man to win Gold medals in both Summer and Winter Games. In 1920 he was light heavyweight boxing Gold medalist and at Lake Placid he was part of the U.S. Gold medal four-man bobsled team.

Eddie Eagan was not the only well known athlete on the four-man American bobsled team. William Fiske was the first American to enlist in the Royal Air Force in World War Two. He was killed when his fighter plane was shot down in the Battle of Britain.

Jay O'Brien, 49, was the oldest Gold Medalist in Winter Games history. He was married to silent screen star Mae Murray.

The fourth team member, British born Clifford "Tippy" Gray, was a songwriter and composed "If You Were The Only Girl In The World."

Canada, represented by a senior club from Winnipeg, won its fourth straight Gold medal but not without a determined run by the U.S. The Winnipegs were a low scoring team but very strong defensively.

The tournament was a double round robin series; each team played each other team twice. Canada defeated the U.S. 2-1 in their first meeting and had a 5-0 record going into their second meeting.

More than 7,000 fans jammed themselves into an indoor arena built to accommodate 3,000. Toronto sportswriter, Lou Marsh, refereed all 12 games.

The U.S. was leading 2-1 with 50 seconds to go when Romeo Rivers rapped a bouncing puck in the net to tie the game.

The teams played three scoreless sudden-death overtime periods without a goal being scored. Had the Americans won, the two teams would have played a third rubber match.

Canada, with a final record of five wins and a tie, was awarded the Gold medal. The United States, with four wins, one loss and a tie, won Silver. Germany with two wins and four losses wound up with Bronze and Poland, with six losses, was the only nation to finish out of the medals. Poland scored only three goals and allowed 34.

Canada scored 32 goals and was scored on only four times; the U.S. had a goals for and against record of 27-5.

Winnipeg's leading scorer was Walter "Pop" Monson with seven goals. He played with Winnipeg when they won the Allan Cup in 1931 and coached Winnipeg Monarchs when they captured the Memorial Cup in 1946.

He played senior hockey in the Maritimes with Glace Bay Miners and Saint John Beavers.

He scored 13 goals in six games with Saint John in 1935 and eight goals in five games with Glace Bay in 1941.

In 1942, when Glace Bay won the Maritime Senior championship, he scored 21 goals in 16 games.

He ended his playing and coaching career with Harringay Racers in the English League.

Ottawa and District hockey executive, Cece Duncan, issued a chilling prophecy at a formal dinner:
*"The time is not too far distant when the greatest hockey opposition will come from European teams. Schools in various countries are teaching pupils the game."*

## OTTAWA ALL STARS

In 1932, a team of Ottawa All-Stars, a collection of players from the Ottawa Senior City League, including 19-year old Bill Cowley, toured Europe.

They visited nine countries, played 35 games, won 32 and tied three. They scored 160 goals and were only scored on 16 times. Louis "Blackie" St. Denis posted 17 shutouts.

The Ottawa All Stars were the first Canadian hockey team to have their games broadcast back home from Europe.

They were the first team to have players' names sewn on the backs of sweaters.

They were the first hockey team to fly. The team flew from Le Bourget, Paris, to Croydon, England, on Air Union's "Golden Ray". The "Golden Ray" carried 12 passengers.

The Ottawa players were not much comforted by the in- flight brochure they were given:
*"Lifebelts under each seat are provided on all aeroplanes crossing the Channel and there is an emergency exit on top of the roof.. To obviate any question of overloading, passengers must be weighed...."*

"Blackie" St. Denis took a turn on the dance floor with figure skating champion, Sonja Henie, in Berlin on Christmas Eve, 1931. She waltzed him around so energetically that he fell into a Christmas tree.

St. Denis played later with the Ottawa Commandos when they won the Allan Cup in 1943 – along with Ken Reardon, Neil Colville, Mac Colville, Alex Shibicky, Ken Kilrea and "Sugar Jim" Henry.

## GARMISCH-PARTENKIRCHEN, 1936

Adolf Hitler was conspicuous at the 1936 Games and patiently signed autographs.

Canada's unbeaten 20-game skein in Olympic play was ended abruptly by a 2-1 loss to Great Britain.

The team from England had one player, defenceman Carl Erhardt, who was 100 percent British.

Of the remaining 10, nine were born in the United Kingdom but moved to Canada as children and learned their hockey here.

The tenth player, Gordon Dailley, was actually born in Canada and served in the Canadian Army.

Part of the folklore of international hockey is the legend that the British coach/manager, crafty and canny John "Bunny" Ahearne, paid clandestine visits to Canada urging players to "come home to play for England."

Canada lodged a protest with the organizing committee but later withdrew it. Canada protested Britain's use of Jimmy Foster and Alex "Sandy" Archer who were ruled to be ineligible by the

International Ice Hockey Federation. In a rare gesture of sportsmanship, Canada unexpectedly withdrew its protest.

Halifax Wolverines, defending Allan Cup champions, were originally slated to represent Canada but withdrew. The substitutes, Allan Cup runners-up, Port Arthur Bearcats, stepped into the breech and were reinforced by players from Halifax and Montreal Royals.

The four Halifax Wolverine players selected asked to be compensated $150 a month for time lost from work. They were dropped from the team. Halifax fans were outraged.

Port Arthur played its first Olympic game in a blinding snowstorm in front of 300 spectators. Sometimes, the puck became lost in snowdrifts.

The Bearcats outscored their opponents 54-7. Great Britain had a goals for and against record of 17-3.

It has yet to be explained why Canada played eight games and Great Britain played only seven.

Great Britain finished the tournament with five wins and two ties for 12 points. Canada finished with seven wins and a loss for 14 points. The Gold Medal was awarded to Great Britain because of its 2-1 win over Canada.

Strange new rules dictated that any team that had beaten another team in a previous round did not have to play that team again in the finals. Thus, rules prevented Canada from playing Britain again in the finals and avenging their 2-1 loss.

The United States, with five wins, two losses, a tie and a goals for and against record of 10-4 wound up with Bronze.

The man who tipped the scales for Great Britain was their goaltender, the great Jimmy Foster.

Born in Glasgow, he moved to Winnipeg with his family as a young boy and played intermediate and senior hockey with Brandon Legion and Winnipeg CPR. His senior league career included stops with Quebec Aces, Glace Bay Miners and North Sydney Victorias.

He played four seasons with Moncton Hawks between 1931 and 1935 and led them to back-to-back Allan Cups in 1933 and 1934. His goals against average hovered between 1.10 and 1.41. In 1933 Moncton Hawks became the first Maritime team to win the Allan Cup.

Jimmy Foster posted two shutout victories over the Saskatoon Quakers in an Allan Cup final series played in Vancouver. The Quakers failed to score a single goal on Foster.

The following year, he was at the top of his form again as Moncton defeated Fort William two games to one in Maple Leaf Gardens.

Ken Farmer, a future President of the Canadian Olympic Association, played for Canada.

One of the on-ice officials in the Allan Cup series was Clarence Campbell who later became President of the National Hockey League.

At the 1936 Olympics Foster posted four shutouts and allowed only three goals in seven games for an incredible goals against average of 0.429. Only '48 Flyer Murray Dowey - with five shutouts and five goals allowed in eight games for a goals against average of .625 – comes close.

Foster capitalized on his Gold Medal performance for England and played three seasons with Harringay Greyhounds in the English League.

The question of amateur/professional status did not arise in 1936. But, it is unlikely Jimmy Foster played senior hockey for Moncton, Quebec, Glace Bay and North Sydney for streetcar fare.

Even though they finished well down in the pack, Italy stunned the United States by scoring a 2-1 upset victory.

Germany finished the tournament in fifth position with a record of three wins, two losses and a tie.

The team's leading player was Rudi Ball, a Jew who fled the country when Hitler's Nazis began their campaign of anti-Semitism.

He was the only Jewish athlete on Germany's Olympic hockey team. Historians believe Ball was an NHL caliber player.

Japan's goaltender, Teiji Honma, caused a sensation when he appeared on the ice wearing a facemask – a first in the history of World and Olympic championship tournaments.

The guns of August, 1939, boomed out the beginning of World War Two. The Olympic Games of 1940 and 1944 were cancelled. The Olympic flame was doused. Athletes of the world would not meet again until 1948 in St. Moritz, Switzerland. Germany and Japan would not be invited to participate.

## TRAIL SMOKE EATERS

With a population of just over 7,500, Trail, B.C. has a rich hockey heritage.

The Senior Trail Smoke Eaters have won two Allan Cups (1938 and 1962) and two World Championships (1939 and 1961).

The Smoke Eaters did not get their name from Cominco's smelters in downtown Trail.

The team received its name in 1929 in a game against Vancouver.

After a questionable penalty call, fans littered the ice with debris. One item thrown at the Trail bench was a pipe, still issuing smoke.

Trail's star center, Carroll Kendall, picked it up and skated onto the ice for his next shift with the pipe clenched between his teeth. A cartoon in a Vancouver paper the next day showed Kendall puffing on a pipe. Vancouver sportswriter A.R. Dingman nicknamed the Trail team "a bunch of smoke-eaters."

They were the very last Canadian amateur squad to win the World crown in 1961.

Trail's cachet was that their teams were populated largely by local players. Imports were a rarity.

In 1944 the Junior Trail Smoke Eaters went to the Memorial Cup finals against defending champion Oshawa Generals. The Smokies were crushed 4-0 by the powerful Generals who were coached by Charlie Conacher.

Oshawa had Floyd Curry, Bill Ezinicki, Harvey Bennett and John Marois in their line-up and added Ted Lindsay, Gus Mortson and David Bauer from St. Mike's College after defeating the Majors.

Trail did not win an Allan Cup in an Olympic year and, therefore, did not get to represent Canada.

Their two Allan Cup victories entitled them to represent Canada twice at World Championships.

Trail won the Allan Cup in 1938 with a three-games-to-one series victory over Cornwall Flyers.

At the 1939 World Championship tournament in Switzerland, the Smokies swept all eight games scoring 42 goals and allowing only one. The only goal given up by Trail came when a defenceman inadvertently shot the puck in his own net in a 2-1 win over the Czechs.

Trail goaltenders "Duke" Scodellaro and "Buck" Buchanan racked up seven shutouts.

During a 55-game European exhibition tour Trail won 53 games, lost one to Wembley All-Stars and tied one 2-2 against Harringay.

The two Trail goaltenders recorded 21 shutouts. Trail scored 301 goals and allowed only 61 goals.

The Smoke Eaters had not been issued traditional Maple Leaf uniforms by the Canadian Amateur Hockey Association prior to their departure for Europe.

They played all their games in Europe with just one set of their orange and black club uniforms – thus becoming the first – and only – Canadian team to wear a hometown uniform.

The Czechs were coached by Trail native Mike Buchna who became known as the father of hockey in Czechoslovakia.

Johnny McCreedy was a member of the 1938-1939 Trail Allan and World Cup teams.

Johnny McCreedy is the only man in hockey history to have his name engraved on Memorial, Allan, Stanley and World championship cups.

He won his Memorial Cup with Winnipeg Monarchs in 1937.

He won Allan Cups with Trail and Kirkland Lake Blue Devils and missed out on a third with Sydney Millionaires.

He won World Cups with Trail and Kirkland Lake and two Stanley Cups with Toronto Maple Leafs. His first Stanley Cup was in 1942 when Toronto became the only team in hockey history to come back from a three game deficit and defeat Detroit Red Wings four games to three.

Johnny McCreedy assisted on Pete Langelle's winning goal at 9.44 of the third period.

When his playing days were over he joined INCO and rose through the ranks to become the company's Chief Executive Officer and Chairman. After his untimely death in 1979 at age 62, INCO renamed its two Levack mines the McCreedy East and McCreedy West Mines.

The Canada Cup was his brainchild. The three feet high, 75-pound stylized half Maple Leaf was cast in solid nickel.

The 1961 World tournament in Geneva was the last ever outdoor tournament played.

Every Smoke Eater player, except one from Fernie, B.C., was a native of Trail.

The seven-game series boiled down to a one-game must win. Because of a 1-1 tie with the Czechs, Trail had to beat Russia by four goals in their final game to edge out Czechoslovakia in goals for and against.

When the final buzzer sounded at 8.30 p.m. Trail coach Bobby Kromm's "Smokies" had defeated Russia 5-1 to win the World Amateur Hockey Championship.

Future NHLer Seth Martin was Trail's goaltender and allowed 12 goals in seven games – four against the U.S., two against Finland and East Germany and one against Sweden, West Germany, Czechoslovakia and Russia. Trail outscored the opposition 45-12.

Seth Martin was selected as best International Ice Hockey Federation goalkeeper in 1961, 1963, 1964 and 1966 and was named to All-Star teams in 1961, 1964 and 1966.

Martin and Czech coach Mike Buckna were both inducted into the IIHF's Hall of Fame.

The 1961 world champions toured Europe, played 26 games, won 22, lost two and tied two.


## "SANDY" WATSON

The late "Sandy" Watson was a unique human being. His velvet voice masked the steel behind it. He was not a man to sit across a table from in a game of five-card stud.

To look at "Sandy" was to conjure up an image of W.C. Fields in his trademark Beaver hat, studying his hand of five Aces in a Mississippi riverboat poker game.

When the Second World War ended, Squadron Leader Alexander Gardner "Sandy" Watson was a 26-year old Senior Medical Officer at Royal Canadian Air Force Headquarters in Ottawa.
He didn't play hockey when he was growing up in Port Dover, Ontario.

"Sandy" was born in Cellardyke, Scotland, near St. Andrews, in 1918. He emigrated to Canada with his parents when he was three. His father built two large commercial boats and fished Lake Ontario.

"Sandy" studied medicine at St. Andrews and later did post-graduate studies at Harvard, Cambridge and Columbia Presbyterian in New York.

He retired from the RCAF as a Group Captain in the 1950s.

He established a practice in ophthalmology in downtown Ottawa and among his patients were seven Prime ministers, two Governors General and their families.

He was a late convert to hockey but quickly became addicted to the sport when he was posted to London.

It was there that he became the manager of an RCAF hockey team and met Frank Boucher.

When he was repatriated home to Ottawa, he became the Manager of the RCAF entry in the four-team Ottawa senior league – Army, RCAF, Hull and the New Edinburgh "Burghs".

On September 8, 1947, he was in his office in Building "B", a temporary wooden wartime building at the corner of Laurier and Elgin Streets.

As he savored his first coffee of the morning, he scanned a morning paper – The Ottawa Journal. What he read made him come "right out of my chair."

A Canadian Press story reported: "Canada, traditionally the world's greatest producer of hockey talent, appears destined for a strictly spectator role when the Olympic hockey championships are held in St. Moritz next February."

In a companion story, Ernie Hamilton, President of the Montreal Royals of the Quebec Senior Hockey League, Allan Cup champions, said that the Royals had declined an invitation to represent Canada.

Hamilton said an Olympic trip "is too costly" and would "disrupt the league schedule".

The Royals had six future Canadiens on their roster – Doug Harvey, Floyd Curry, Howard Riopelle, Tod Campeau, Gerry McNeil and Jacques Locas.

44

What was left unsaid was the fact that Canada could not provide a team that could satisfy the Olympic fiction of "amateur" status.

Ottawa Citizen Sportswriter, Jack Koffman, wrote on October 16, 1947, that to "satisfy Olympic amateur standards, Canada would have to send a juvenile or midget team."

Olympic amateur standards were a farce and were accorded lip service around the world. Even at the first championships in Antwerp, the United States team's roster included a professional.

Gerry "Duke" Geran, a Dartmouth College star, played four games in the NHL with Montreal Wanderers. He also played semi-pro in Boston. After the Olympics, he played with Paris Volants. The balance of his NHL career was 33 games with Boston Bruins in 1925-26.

In 1948, United States team members were paid a weekly salary. Even the second team the U.S. Olympic Committee sent over in 1948 was given modest per diem walking around money.

International hockey ceased being a showcase for amateurs when Czechoslovakia and Russia burst on the scene. The players were full-time hockey players in the armed forces and their salaries were paid by the military.

During the 1955 World Championships, a passport check revealed that 10 Canadian players listed "hockey player" as their occupation. Some of the players who suited up for Canada over the years were household names on strong senior teams across Canada. All of them were paid weekly salaries on a par with NHL levels.

Senior leagues across Canada attempted to cap their payrolls by limiting the number of "imports" a team could carry on its roster.

45

The "imports" were paid handsomely and some were given "day jobs" where little was expected of them.

Some players on farm teams in the old Quebec Senior League actually prayed the parent NHL club would not call them up. If they were called up they might have to take pay cuts and lose some of the perqs their senior team provided.

Tommy Gorman's senior Ottawa Senators always traveled First Class on trains – roomettes, Club Car, superior meal service – and players were expected to wear suits, shirts and neckties.

"Sandy" Watson's first impulse, after he read the newspaper article, was to phone George Dudley in Midland, Ontario. Dudley was Secretary Registrar of the Canadian Amateur Hockey Association.

"Sandy" introduced himself, explained he had read the article and asked if a team from the RCAF would be acceptable.

George Dudley quickly agreed that a team from the RCAF would be welcome. But, he cautioned "Sandy" that he had only 48 hours to confirm. That was the deadline "Bunny" Ahearne of the International Ice Hockey Federation had imposed on the CAHA.

"Sandy" was "only a lowly Squadron Leader" but he had clout other Squadron Leaders did not enjoy. He was the personal physician to Air Marshal Wilf Curtis, Chief of the Air Staff. He was also the family doctor for Mrs. Curtis and the Curtis children.

"Sandy's" immediate superior, Air Commodore Dave MacKell, had been a prominent Ottawa athlete who had been associated on the sidelines with the Ottawa Rough Riders football team and the Ottawa RCAF Flyers, 1942 Allan Cup champions.

"Sandy" Watson and Dave MacKell took the proposal to the Chief of the Air Staff and, within hours, they were in the office of Defence Minister Brooke Claxton.

The Montreal Minister was a rabid Canadiens' fan and a prominent member and supporter of the Montreal Amateur Athletic Union.

He gave his immediate OK.

The Flyers were in.

George Dudley was so advised before the end of the workday.

That left "Sandy" with several immediate problems. He didn't have a team; he didn't have a single piece of equipment and he had only slightly more than three months to ice an entry.

Air Marshall Curtis called "Sandy" in and pledged the full support of the RCAF. He said that every resource the RCAF possessed was behind him and at his disposal – every resource except money. His reasoning was that if the team crapped out he wasn't keen on Questions in the House of Commons criticizing the Department of National Defence for wasting public money.

One of "Sandy's" strong suits was that he was THE consummate optimist. He never took "NO" for an answer. He also had more nerve than an open tooth. In any Hollywood movie about a Prisoner of War camp, "Sandy" would have been cast as "The Scrounger".

"I was wet behind the ears. I was a novice. I was new at the game. I was greener than grass. I didn't know any better. Boy, did I sure learn fast. I was so bold. I went to hockey equipment manufacturers, cold turkey, and asked them to donate sticks and equipment.

"CCM equipped every player with top of the line Tackaberry skates. In those days, 'Tacks' didn't come with sewn-in tendon guards so the boys took their skates to Hackett's Shoe Repair Shop on Bank Street in Ottawa and had them sewn on.

"I believe that Hackett's were the very first shoemaker to sew in tendon guards. Later, they were standard on all hockey skates sold.

"Northland gave us 300 sticks. We came back home with one – a much taped-over goalie's stick that Murray Dowey used to rack up five shutouts.

"Spalding outfitted every player from the skin out with every piece of equipment – sweaters, stockings, shin pads, elbow pads, jocks, cups, garter belts, braces, shoulder pads, pants and gloves.

"Every Canadian manufacturer cooperated and donated without a moment's hesitation.

"So far, I hadn't spent a nickel of the RCAF's money.

"Air Marshall Curtis called me in and said he had one favor to ask. He asked me if it would be possible to incorporate an RCAF roundel as a crest on team sweaters.

"So, I mocked up a sweater and took it to Toronto. The Canadian Olympic Association was being meeting at the Royal York Hotel.

"Sidney Dawe was the Canadian Olympic Association President and he told the representatives of 16 sports assembled around a long table that he had one item of New Business that did not appear on their agenda.

"He told me to 'show them the sweater' and then he did a whip-around the table.

It was a powder-blue coloured sweater with the distinctive RCAF bulls-eye roundel as the sweater's crest.

"The comments were all negative like 'we can't have a roundel on our Olympic sweater' or 'we can't have this' or 'they are going to have to wear the red Maple Leaf like other members of our Olympic team'.

"Everybody pooh-poohed the sweater. One of them said: 'Mr. Dawe, this is the Olympics. We are not putting on a show for the RCAF. If the RCAF wants this sweater, let them showcase it somewhere else'.

"Sidney Dawe heard everyone out. Then, he turned to his recording secretary and told her: 'take down this resolution. The Canadian Olympic Association has accepted the RCAF sweater'.

"I was stunned. I was amazed. He was a no nonsense guy. He was tough. He was the head of Atlas Construction in Montreal. And, that's how the team came to wear Air Force blue and the RCAF roundel.

"I left the Royal York and went to a pay-phone. I called Air Marshall Curtis and he said: 'where are you'? I told him I was in Toronto at a meeting of the Olympic committee and then I could barely contain myself. I blurted out 'we won. The RCAF sweater and roundel will be worn for the Olympic Games'."

"Sandy" and Coach Frank Boucher were a seamless team and they never crossed swords. "Sandy" ran the administrative end off-ice and Frank ran the team on-ice.

"Of course, he consulted me when we were trying to put a team together".

Their next assignment together was to attempt to cobble a silk purse from a sow's ear – pick the RCAF's best for a hockey team to compete with the best at the world amateur level.

The RCAF flew prospects to Ottawa in waves for tryouts and quartered them in Princess Louise barracks in downtown Ottawa.

"Princess Louise barracks should have been out-fitted with a revolving door.

"God, they were awful! They were pathetic. The press was patient at first but then they turned their siege guns on us. It got so bad that I stopped giving interviews. The only man I continued to talk to was the late Tom Foley at CFRA.

"But, the show had to go on. One of the memories I still feel badly about is Ottawa hockey player, Hughie Riopelle. Tommy Gorman mentioned him to me. He said: 'He's good enough to play in the NHL. Why don't you get in touch with him and get him to join the team'?

"Hughie was an 18-year old scoring sensation with St. Pat's in the Ottawa junior league. I think he had 30 goals in 30 games. Hughie's main competitor for the league scoring title that year was Larry Reagan who was with the Ottawa Junior Senators. Reagan later made NHL history when he became the oldest rookie, at age 26, to win the Calder Trophy with Boston Bruins.

"Before we could move on Hughie, the Athletic Director at St. Pat's, Father Peake, an Oblate priest, called me and asked why we would want to invite Hughie to join a team 'not considered a team worthy of going to the Olympics'. He said Hughie would lose his school year. He said we would be ruining a young man's career. He said we would ruin his life. He said Hughie would turn out to be a bum.

"Frank and I said to one another: 'Let's not touch him'. I never, ever saw him play but years later I met him and told him what the Athletic Director had said and done. He was stunned; he was angry; he was crushed. Hughie had a great career in the Quebec Senior League but he would have jumped at the opportunity to play with the Flyers. I guess the Athletic Director had one eye on the upcoming playoffs and didn't want to part with his top scorer".

After his playing days with the Ottawa Senators were over, Hughie Riopelle enjoyed a successful career as an extremely popular public relations officer for Air Canada in Ottawa. He is one of Ottawa's top amateur golfers and a frequent partner of former Prime Minister Jean Chretien.

"Sandy" Watson was a scrapper to the very end. He died at his Rockcliffe home on December 28, 2003, still fighting the cancer that had invaded his body 18 months earlier.

Sitting across from him in the sunroom of his home he gave me hours of interview time and never once did he mention that an inoperable cancer was slowly winning the battle for his life.

"Sandy" never gave up on life. Doctors told him his last resort was "pain management" but that diagnosis didn't mesh with his expectations. He was in and out of hospital several times for various surgical procedures which seemed to give him a second wind, if ever so briefly.

Ottawa Flyers Ab Renaud and Ted Hibberd attended "Sandy's" Visitation in a downtown Ottawa funeral home. Andre Laperriere drove up from snowbound Montreal, extended his condolences to "Sandy's" widow, Pat, and his two sons, John and Alex. Then, he jumped back in his car and drove home to Outrement.

Barbara Ann Scott's and her husband, Tom King's floral tribute called "Sandy" a "visionary."

## FRANK BOUCHER

Flyers' Coach Frank Boucher was a second-generation member of the hockey playing Boucher dynasty. His father, George (Buck) and three of his uncles played in the National Hockey League.

Frank never made it to the Big Show. His professional career in North America was with New York Rovers, Providence and Philadelphia. In 1938, New York Rovers won the U.S. national title.

He was born in Ottawa on March 3, 1918. In 1931 he was a member of an Ottawa team that won the city midget title. Playing with Lisgar Collegiate, he was a member of two Eastern Ontario championship teams.

In 1942 he played with Eastern Canadian Allan Cup finalists, RCAF Flyers.

Frank remembers his very first American Hockey League game as if it were yesterday: "I took a terrific hit from Eddie Shore".

Frank's father, George (Buck) played four seasons of senior hockey with the New Edinburghs in Ottawa. He played 13 NHL seasons with Ottawa Senators, three with Montreal Maroons and one with Chicago Black Hawks.

He was a 169-pound defenceman who scored 117 goals in 449 NHL games and five more during playoffs.

Frank's uncle, Frank, is a hockey legend. He won the Lady Byng Trophy seven times in eight years. The League presented him with the original cup and commissioned a copy.

Uncle Frank Boucher joined the Northwest Mounted Police when he was 17. He bought his way off the force for $50 to play professional hockey. He played three seasons with Ottawa New Edinburghs and four with Vancouver Millionaires.

He spent his entire NHL career with New York Rangers – 12 as a player and five as a coach. He scored 161 goals in 557 games and assisted on 262 for a career points total of 423. He also scored 20 times in 16 playoff games.

His nickname was "Raffles" after the gentleman thief – a tribute to his clean play and puck-stealing ability. He averaged one penalty a season over four seasons and two penalties in two other seasons.

Frank Boucher was the first coach to pull his goaltender for an extra skater. He developed the box defence to kill penalties. In 1942, he advocated adding the red line to speed up play.

Nephew Frank Boucher joined the Royal Canadian Air Force in 1942 and was a Sergeant when he received "the call" to coach Canada's entry in the 1948 Olympic Games in St. Moritz.

When the war ended in 1945, Frank was stationed in London.

"Waiting to be repatriated to Canada were a number of established hockey players stationed at the many RCAF and Army units in England. With these players, teams were formed and a league organized. It included RCAF and Army teams and a local team made up of players who had played in the pre-war English League.

"Games were played at the Empire Pool to sell-out crowds.

"Our team, RCAF HQs, with Bobby Lee running it, eventually won the championship, due in part to repatriations plus having Johnny Mowers in our goal. Along the way we had an RCAF Medical Officer, "Sandy" Watson as the team doctor.

"Through this association, he became very interested in hockey. As more players were repatriated, we finally ended up with a combined team, Air Force and Army, only. Some of the players were Johnny Mowers, Bob Whitelaw, Hub Macey, Norm Tustin, Tony Licari, Jack Portland, Jack Schmidt and Gene Rheinhart.

"The team was under Army control with a Brigadier MacDonald in charge. On trips to France and Switzerland we had "Sandy" Watson and "Cab" Calloway looking out for RCAF interests."

In February, 1946, a team run by Frank Boucher and "Sandy" Watson traveled to Zurich and Basel and defeated the Swiss national squad. In April, 1946, they defeated a Czech team at Wembley. They then defeated the Canadian Army team to win the inter-service championship.

The friendly relationship between Frank Boucher and "Sandy" Watson had a lasting impact. In 1948 when "Sandy" was looking for a Coach, there was no short list. Frank Boucher was always his first and only choice.

Air Commodore Dave MacKell said: "Mind you, we'd like to have a name coach but the feeling is that the man should come from within the service".

"Sandy" was aware of my hockey background and also that I was clued in on ice hockey in Europe. Friends of mine from Ottawa (Ed Mentzel, Ed Gromoli, Tommy McIntyre and Charlie Hulquist) played for the Prague Lawn Tennis Club in 1934-35. Players from the pre-war English League also passed on helpful advice.

"Both 'Sandy' and I ended up at Air Force Headquarters in Ottawa in the summer of 1946. We were both associated with local RCAF teams in Ottawa".

Sports writers across Canada went into a guessing game, speculating over who the Coach of the '48 Flyers would be.

The odds-on favorite was Mervyn "Red" Dutton, a former National Hockey League President who had played 449 games on defence over 10 NHL seasons with Montreal Maroons and New York Americans. He had also coached New York Americans.

Had "Red" Dutton been chosen for the coaching assignment there would have been few complaints, if any, because he lost two sons serving in the RCAF during World War Two.

Frank Boucher was given the unenviable task of cobbling together a world-class senior team, all amateurs, in but a few weeks.

He describes the initial try-outs as "terrible, terrible."

Even though the word went out to all RCAF stations to "send us your best – players who have played at Junior A and Senior levels" – the pickings were slim.

"One player who probably knew he was about to be cut came to me and said he was not playing up to scratch because his skates were specially sharpened for outdoor rinks only".

Frank had scouting reports on European teams the Flyers would face from Canadians playing in Europe.

""Bunny" Ahearne's advice to me was not to give up goals – 'win a game 1-0. Don't even think about winning 5-3 or 7-4 – it's the goals against that will kill you and decide a tie situation'."

Frank's defensive strategy was already set before he boarded the Queen Elizabeth in New York

– "the defencemen play back, one fore checker chases the puck carrier and the two other forwards pick up the wings".

He chuckles, as he reminisced with me in his Mountain farmhouse just outside Ottawa more than 50 years later.

"I think that today they call my strategy 'the trap'."

After the 1948 Olympics, Frank's RCAF posting took him to London. For four years, between 1949 and 1953, he was the playing manager of Wembley Lions who won the English national title in 1952.

Frank was a favorite of Wembley owner Sir Arthur Elvins who would send his personal car and driver to transport Frank to practices and games.

On top of his RCAF salary, Sir Arthur paid Frank the unheard of weekly salary of 100 Pounds Sterling.

"Sandy" Watson maintains that when Sir Arthur died, Frank Boucher was remembered significantly in his Will.

Frank came home to Canada to an RCAF posting and coached a senior team in Belleville in 1954. From 1955 to 1968 he was playing coach of RCAF teams. He retired from the RCAF in 1966 and began a second career as an accountant with an Ottawa area pulp and paper company.

In 1969, he was the business manager for Ottawa based Team Canada.

A widower, Frank lived alone with his beloved cat, "Rusty", in a wooden farmhouse on his family's 75-acre farm in Mountain, south of Ottawa. His daughter, Diane, lived just a couple of farms away down a gravel road.

Frank and "Sandy" Watson were born three weeks apart and they died two weeks apart. Frank was 85 when he passed away on December 12, 2003.

Frank was in denial in his final weeks on earth. He refused to accept the fact he was suffering from throat cancer. He dismissed his affliction as "a sore throat".

We sat in his living room with a tape recorder on a small table between us. When I played the tapes back to transcribe them, my voice was loud and clear. Frank's was inaudible.

His voice was so low and so raspy it would not register on the tape recorder only a few feet away from him.

## JAMES P. (JIM) McCAFFREY

Jim McCaffrey was another charter member of the "Brains Trust" that assembled the final Flyers' hockey team.

Jim was a Lacrosse star with Ottawa's only Mann Cup winner, the 1922 Emmets.

He enjoyed a long and illustrious career as a manager and team executive with Ottawa hockey, football and baseball teams for 40 years. He was associated with Allan Cup and Grey Cup championship teams.

Jim McCaffrey was a longtime business associate of T.P. Gorman who owned the Ottawa Auditorium and the Ottawa Senators of the Quebec Senior Hockey League.

His wise counsel and acute hockey judgment were invaluable to "Sandy" Watson and Frank Boucher.

## BARBARA ANN SCOTT

Barbara Ann Scott was the RCAF Flyers' "Good Luck" charm.

When her own skating schedule allowed, she was on or near the players' bench cheering her hometown hockey heroes on.

She was there when the Flyers received their Gold Medals and they were there when she received hers.

Barbara Ann Scott swept through Europe like a whirlwind.

Her father, Lieutenant Colonel Clyde Rutherford Scott, was severely wounded and left for dead on the battlefield of St. Julien in April, 1915. His body was literally riddled with shrapnel and machine gun and small arms bullets.

He spent the next two years as a Prisoner of War in a German hospital in Heidelberg. Two years after he had been given up for dead by his parents, he came home to Ottawa.

The army rated Colonel Scott 75 percent incapacitated but he soldiered on, serving four Defence Ministers as an advisor. His war wounds hastened his premature death in 1941.

Clyde Rutherford lived long enough to see Barbara Ann win the Canadian Junior figure skating championship when she was only 11. But, he did not live to see her conquer Canada, North America, Europe, the World and the Olympics.

Barbara Ann's husband, Tommy King, places her achievements in perspective: "Tiger" Woods won the world's top four golfing titles but it took him a whole calendar year. "Barb won the Canadian, North American, European, World and Olympic titles in the span of just a couple of months."

When her father died, money was very tight in the Scott household. Ottawa friends raised $10,000 to send her, her mother, Mary, and her coach, Sheldon Galbraith, to the European championships in Davos, Switzerland and the World championships in Stockholm, Sweden. Winning the World's, six of the eight judges placed her First and two awarded her 6.0 – perfect scores.

When she successfully defended her World title in Prague in 1948, she recorded the highest scores ever on a Prague rink. She defeated 18 competitors from five nations to defend her European title.

At the 1948 St. Moritz Olympics, she skated 13th in a field of 25 – exactly in the middle. The ice was badly chewed up by a hockey game that had been played that same morning. She skated against four national champions – England, Austria, Hungary and Czechoslovakia.

Barbara Ann, her mother and her coach walked every inch of the ice surface to check it for ruts and crevasses. Other skaters also shared invaluable intelligence about ice conditions.

Barbara Ann blew the competition away. Eight of the nine judges awarded her Firsts. Eva Pawlik of Austria was runner-up with Silver and Jeanette Altwegg of Great Britain won Bronze.

A magazine writer reported Barbara Ann was so far ahead after the compulsory figures she could have fallen down four times and still won.

At the age of 19, she had done it all – Canadian Junior champion, six Canadian senior championships, three North American titles, back-to-back European and World crowns and Olympic Gold. In 1945, 1947 and 1948, Canadian sportswriters voted her the Lou Marsh Trophy as Canada's most outstanding athlete. Toronto Argonaut football player, Joe Krol, edged her out in voting in 1946.

She turned professional in 1949 and skated in ice revues until she became weary of travel and "living out of suitcases."

Barbara Ann Scott married American Tom King in Toronto in a storybook wedding in Toronto in 1955 to settle down in "that little white cottage with a picket fence."

Tom King was an All-American basketball player at Michigan and played pro ball with Chicago and Detroit.

He became a publicist with the Wirtz Entertainment empire where he met Barbara Ann.

Later he joined the Kennedy family and became second-in-command to Kennedy son-in-law Sargent Schriver, the CEO of the Chicago Trade Mart, the largest retail operation under one roof in the world. When Schriver retired, Tom succeeded him in the top job.

He served during World War 2 as a Marine Corps Captain.

He is also an accomplished amateur musician and, together with a half-dozen retired Chicago businessmen, has produced seven CDs of easy-listening, "1930s' Chicago jazz."

The CDs drew the notice of a major music distributor and "Tom King and The Royal Chicagoans" are being sold around the world. All royalties are donated to medical charity.

The Kings lived in Chicago until they moved to Amelia Island on the Georgia-Florida border.

They live with their three cats – Tomcat, Sir Nigel and Jennifer – and Barb feeds an army of feral cats, turtles, possums and armadillos.

Barb has never forgotten her hardscrabble youth when the family lived on Colonel Scott's $3,000 annual pension.

When she was 10, her mother took her to New York to be fitted with her first pair of Gustav Stanzione boots. The boots cost $25 a pair and were the best money could buy. Gustav Stanzione told Barb's mother that her foot would not grow much more than a half-size thereafter. "And, they didn't."

She also had a pair of Wilson blades from England and "they cost $15. I wore them all through my amateur and professional skating careers."

Following her conquering skates through Europe, she came home to Ottawa and a crowd estimated as high as 100,000 lined the streets to salute her.

The City of Ottawa tried to present her with a Buick convertible (License Plate # 47 U 1). But, the gift would have compromised her amateur status and she had to decline the gift. The City of Ottawa put the car in mothballs and, after she turned professional, they had the Canary Yellow car painted Powder Blue and fitted it out with License Plate # 48 U 1.

Reliable Toys introduced Barbara Ann Scott dolls and, priced at $5.95, they flew off the shelves. Today, should you be lucky enough to find one on eBay, the price is US$750.00.

Barbara Ann formed the St. Lawrence Foundation to share part of her earnings from all sources with disabled children in Canada.

When the Kings were in Ottawa for the 100th birthday of Minto Skating Club, Barbara Ann told the closing Black Tie dinner: "Ottawa is my home,

Canada is my country and Minto is my Club." In the lowest of low-key announcements, Tom thanked the dinner guests for the hospitality and warm reception and tossed out a throwaway line: "By the way, Barb and I have donated $100,000 to the Minto Skating Club for scholarships and the money is in their bank account."

In 1939, when King George V1 and Queen Elizabeth paid the first visit ever to Canada by a Royal Family, the Province of New Brunswick hosted a luncheon at St. Andrews-by-the-sea. Royal Doulton was commissioned to produce an 84-piece China Service for 12.

Each piece had the provenance fired in the glaze – venue, date, occasion. Each piece bore the Royal Cipher and the Coat of Arms of New Brunswick.

Nine years later, Barbara Ann skated a benefit in St Andrews and the town's Mayor, the Premier and the Lieutenant Governor presented her with the China service.

Recently, she decided it was time for the China to "go home" and donated it to the Lieutenant Governor's residence.

An appraiser placed an "arbitrary value of $50,000" on the gift. He added: "It's priceless. A serious collector might pay $100,000 for it."

Barbara Ann keeps on giving and giving – never forgetting how much was given to her in her youth.

She never passes up an invitation to "come home" to Canada to help figure skating any way she can – coaching, judging or just being a presence at national and international competitions.

And, she has never broken her half-century-plus connection with the RCAF Flyers.

## JOHN FRANCIS "BUNNY" AHEARNE

Once the Flyers stepped on the gangplank of the ocean liner Queen Elizabeth in New York, "Bunny" Ahearne "owned" them.

He was their travel agent, their booking agent and their paymaster – except, as true amateurs, they were not paid. He booked and paid for their transportation and accommodation. Except for their lodgings in St. Moritz, the Flyers were booked in fleabag hotels. "Bunny" could find more than four ways to cut corners from a square.

"Bunny could skin a flea for the tallow."

The Flyers found themselves always roughing it in digs that were just a notch up or down from logging camp barracks.

John Francis "Bunny" Ahearne never played a game of hockey in his life but, through the sheer force of personality and a gift of organizational skills, he became the most powerful man in amateur hockey in the world.

Born in Kinnagh, Wexford, Ireland, in 1901 he volunteered to serve in the British army in World War One. One of his first jobs after the war was with a London travel agency and, within a year, he opened his own agency.

He saw his first game of hockey at Golders Green rink in north London in 1931 and immediately saw the potential of the sport and a link with his travel agency.

He was named Assistant Secretary of the British Ice Hockey Association in 1933 and the following year became Secretary. He held the post for 38 years until 1971 when he became President, a post he held for 11 years until his retirement in 1982.

He represented Great Britain on the International Ice Hockey Federation for 40 years.

Al Eagleson told me "Bunny" ran the IIHF "like a little fiefdom. He took a Mickey Mouse organization and made it into a world power house".

Al Eagleson said: "I met him for the first time in 1969 and he was reluctant to meet me. He said he didn't want to have anything to do with a union leader. But, the meeting took place and we hit it off right away.

"'Bunny' was anti-Canada and he saw the National Hockey League as his opponent. But, he was a doer, a risk taker and he wasn't afraid to put his money where his mouth was to make things happen."

And happen they did.

From the time the RCAF Flyers boarded their ship in New York until they arrived back home, "Bunny" Ahearne was their minder. He organized their 34-game exhibition tour through Europe, gambled the front money and orchestrated all hotel and travel reservations.

When the Flyers arrived in London, Ahearne had some bad news for "Sandy" Watson. The Flyers' poor press notices had preceded them and European teams wanted to cancel exhibition games with them.

The lopsided exhibition losses to McGill University and Bill Cowley's Ottawa Army squad spooked them into believing the Flyers were a team of stiffs who wouldn't draw flies. As Yogi Berra said decades later – fans would stay away in droves.

Part of the Flyers' folklore – a legend – is that George Mara was present when Ahearne advised

"Sandy" that the exhibition schedule would have to be slashed drastically.

This was devastating news as "Sandy" was counting on the Flyers' cut of box office receipts to subsidize their 75-day barnstorming tour. The Flyers intended to sing for their suppers.

Flyer George Mara was the scion of a wealthy Toronto wine and spirits importing family. He was not born with a silver spoon in his mouth; the spoon was gold.

George allegedly asked: "How much do you stand to lose, Mr. Ahearne?"

The reply was: "I will be in hock for $32,000. That's the total amount of the seed money I'll have to put up front."

George Mara didn't bat an eyelash. He merely said: "Well, then, why don't I just stroke you a cheque for that amount right now?!"

The complete tour was reinstated immediately. George Mara will neither confirm nor deny the anecdote. He just laughs.

The Flyers played 42 games in seven countries won 31, lost five and tied six, traveled 15,000 miles and played in front of 250,000 spectators. They lost only one game to a national team – an exhibition game against the Swiss national team. Their four other exhibition losses were to European teams composed almost entirely of Canadians.

When it was all over, "Bunny" Ahearne reported to the Canadian Amateur Hockey Association that the Flyers' tour cost 9,000 Pounds Sterling or $36,000 and small change Canadian. When hockey people discuss "Bunny" Ahearne, there are no shades of gray – only black and white; you either love him or loathe him. His name evokes strong emotions.

George Mara calls him "a crook" and said "I wouldn't have anything to do with him."

"Sandy" Watson and Flyers' coach Frank Boucher were foursquare in "Bunny's" corner and swore by him. Shortly after their arrival in London, "Bunny" asked "Sandy" and Frank if he could address a team meeting in the Crofton Hotel in Kensington.

He told the players that if teams wound up in a dead heat in games won and lost, medal winners would be decided by goals for divided by goals against.

Therefore, a team that scored 40 goals and allowed 20 would have a quotient of 2.

A team that scored 25 goals and allowed six would have a winning quotient of 4.1666.

In the end, "Bunny's" words were prophetic. Canada and Czechoslovakia ended the 1948 tourney with identical records – seven wins and a tie.

Czechoslovakia scored 80 goals but allowed 18. Their quotient was 4.44.

Canada scored 69 times but allowed only five goals so their final quotient was 13.8.

On the basis of the higher number, Canada was awarded Gold.

"Sandy" Watson describes "Bunny's" remarks to the Flyers as "brilliant. He walked us through the realities of international hockey, the rules, and the referees, what penalties they'd call.

"As it turned out, they called everything. If our puck carrier brushed by an opponent on a rush they'd charge him with rough play or interference or some such nonsensical penalty.

He gave us the best advice we ever had. He said the main thing was to win a game 1-0 rather than

23-6. Don't let the other side score. You'll win on goals scored against and that's how we won.

"He was a super character. The International Ice Hockey Federation were a bunch of jerks. He was only the Secretary but he ran the whole bloody show."

Frank Boucher liked Ahearne because he ran a tight ship and got things done. He remembers attending one meeting when Ahearne arrived late half drunk: "He quickly got the agenda back on the rails. He said to one guy, an IIHF executive member, a Belgian: 'sit down, shut up, and shut your mouth. You don't even have a goddamn team.' The Belgian guy shut up and sat down."

"Sandy's" rosy vision of Ahearne may have been clouded by the fact "Bunny" was on the hook for all the bills – travel, hotels, and meals. It relieved "Sandy" of a potentially worrisome responsibility.

"Sandy" says: "if we had lost and blew a wad of public funds there would have been hell to pay back in Ottawa – Questions in the House, nasty editorials and columns. I was only 26 at the time. I was a novice. I was new at the game but, boy, did I ever learn a lot fast."

I said to "Sandy": "you must have stayed in the odd fleabag hotel. He shot back: "they were all fleabag hotels. You have to remember this was just after the war and much of England and the continent had been destroyed by bombing raids."

Nevertheless, "Bunny" Ahearne's expense budget made no allowances for Five Star accommodations.

Ahearne invited the Flyers to his London flat for a social evening and Ab Renaud remembers that "the obvious trappings of wealth blinded" him.

"Mrs. Ahearne was dripping with jewels and she was wearing the latest fashions."

It is true that "Bunny" Ahearne capitalized on his executive role with the IIHF.

No hockey player in Europe moved unless the travel arrangements were made through Ahearne's travel agency. But, Ahearne gambled with his own money and if a tour bombed there was no Guardian Angel in the wings to bail him out or compensate him.

"Sandy" also volunteered that there was no one else who could have organized an exhibition tour through seven sets of customs and immigration borders.

He said he asked Ottawa Senators' owner, T.P. Gorman, if he thought he could lay on arrangements from Canada.

"Tommy just shook his head and said 'no way'. He said he'd have to be part magician to deal with all the red tape and paper work that was especially complicated by currency restrictions in almost every country. I have no idea how "Bunny" could get his money out of Czechoslovakia, for example."

"Sandy" may also have taken a shine to "Bunny" Ahearne because they shared a lot in common. They were both doers - "hustlers who got things done" – and neither one ever came to a corner he couldn't cut.

"Bunny" Ahearne elevated European hockey from laughable Club team competition into major sporting events. He was early to recognize the cash-cow potential of television and he played a major role in negotiating profitable broadcasting rights. He was also in the vanguard of marketers who pioneered selling advertising panels on rink boards.

Probably, more than any other one man,

"Bunny" Ahearne oversaw the growth of international hockey.

He died in England in April, 1985.

He was elected to the British Hockey Hall of Fame in 1865, to Canada's Hockey Hall of Fame in 1977 and the IIHF Hall of Fame in 1997.


## THE REVOLVING DOOR

T.P. (Tommy) Gorman was Ottawa's best known and most respected sports promoter.

He was involved with hockey, lacrosse, baseball, harness racing and figure skating.

He was an Olympian in 1908 – a member of Canada's national lacrosse team. He either coached or managed seven Stanley Cup championship teams.

Tommy Gorman was one of a very few whose faith in the Flyers never wavered. After the Flyers played their last exhibition game against a strong Belleville Intermediate team before leaving for Europe he told "Sandy" Watson "the boys are ready. They are going to bring home Gold Medals".

Tommy Gorman owned both the Ottawa Auditorium and the Ottawa Senators senior hockey club.

He donated the rink to the Flyers for twice a day tryouts and practices and was always on hand if "Sandy" Watson or Frank Boucher and his father, George "Buck" Boucher, needed an outside opinion.

"Sandy" Watson says: "we had at least 25 rinks after us to use their facilities. The Auditorium was the top facility in the area and it was just a short walk to and from the players' barracks."

With hindsight, perhaps "Tommy" Gorman

should have installed a revolving door on the Auditorium.

"Sandy" Watson put out the word to RCAF bases across Canada to send players with Junior "A" or Senior hockey experience to Ottawa for tryouts: "Send us your very best!"

"Sandy" Watson's assessment of the hopefuls – "awful, they were just awful. I thought if we took a team to Europe made up of the airmen who tried out, I'd have to come back home on a slow banana boat by way of South America.

"Connie Tudin and Stan Rooke from Ottawa were in the RCAF but they had signed professional contracts and were not eligible. Three of the top professional players in the entire world were ex-RCAF but they were starring on the same line with Boston Bruins. Milt Schmidt, Bobby Bauer and "Woody" Dumart, the fabled Kraut Line, played on the RCAF Flyers club that won the Allan Cup in 1942."

Only eight players – Louis Lecompte, Patsy Guzzo, Roy Forbes, Ross King, Hubie Brooks, "Red" Gravelle, Irving Taylor and Andy Gilpin survived from Day One to the final 17 picks.

In between, Frank Boucher and his father, George "Buck" auditioned:

Sergeant John Frenette who played on an Allan Cup championship team in 1941-42 with Ottawa RCAF.

Corporal Jack Seymour who also played on the 1941-42 Allan Cup team.

Flight Lieutenant Jack Maitland who played with Winnipeg Elmwoods when they won the Memorial Cup.

LAC Oscar Kleppe who was a journeyman

senior player with Saskatoon.

Sergeant Lionel Bergeron, RCAF, Winnipeg, who played with the University of Ottawa and the Montreal Junior Canadiens team that lost out to Montreal Royals in a Memorial Cup semi-final series.

Flying Officer Bert Paxton who played for the Senior Calgary Stampeders. Goaltender Paxton was Coach Boucher's first choice for back-up goalie but he disqualified himself. He said he could not sign the Olympic amateur Oath because he had been paid as a professional.

Flight Lieutenant W. McLeod, Toronto.

LAC Frank G. Hammond, Montreal Junior Canadiens.

LAC Howard Kelly, Barrie.

Sergeant H. Sergent, Trenton.

Sergeant D. Sherman, Trenton, played Junior and Senior hockey in Ottawa.

Flying Officer T.G. (Tommy) Moore, Montreal, older brother of Canadiens' star and league leading scorer Dickie Moore.

Eric Milford

Stan Molinski

Flying Officer Eric McNeely who played Junior and senior hockey in Ottawa.

Flying Officer Larry Gibson.

Corporal John Leminchick, Renfrew.

Flight Sergeant Al Darlington.

Fred Hector.

"Dode" Clarke.

Tom Deacon.

Aurele Legris.

LAC Joe Evans who played Junior and Senior in Montreal and Halifax.

Warrant Officer Gordon Ault who played with

Halifax Crescents, Hull Volants and Ottawa
Montagnards.
Ross Waugh.
Gus Baudais.
George Wilson.
Al Lavery.
Larry Paget.
Chuck Rafuse.
Doug Lyon who played in 1942-43 with the
Maritime Senior champions.
Trev Williams.
Robbie Robson.

Coach Boucher's original lineup included
eight Day One players plus Jack Seymour, Stan
Molinski, Jack Maitland, Len Beatch, Dick Thomas
and Tommy Moore. He also added Ben Ethier from
Sudbury.

On November 15, the team played an RCAF
team from Trenton and won 7-4. Patsy Guzzo and
Andy Gilpin both scored twice and "Red" Gravelle,
Tommy Moore and Hubie Brooks added singles.

On November 16 they played Queen's
University and won 8-5. Len Beatch and Jack
Seymour both scored twice and Stan Rooke, Tommy
Moore, "Red" Gravelle and Hubie Brooks potted
singles.

On November 25, Coach Boucher's lineup
included Trev Williams and Ross King in nets,
Seymour, Molinski and Maitland on defence and
Beatch, Moore and Thomas on forward lines.

On December 10, the coach added Louis
Bergeron and George Wilson to the line-up.

## FIRST HOMETOWN EXHIBITION GAME

On December 13, the Flyers took to the ice for their first exhibition game before hometown fans. The Auditorium was packed to the rafters with 6,500-plus fans. Frank Boucher added a new goaltender, Joe Tunney, to his lineup.

The opposition was McGill University and the United States Olympic team had beaten the Redmen rather badly.

The Redmen whipped the Flyers 7-0.

The goaltender for McGill was Toronto born Jack Gelineau who would later win the Calder Trophy as Rookie of the Year with Boston Bruins.

Despite the lopsided score, Ottawa Journal sports reporter Tommy Shields credited Tunney with keeping the score down.

Sportswriters began to cock their weapons. They had already loaded live rounds.

Ottawa Citizen writer Jack Koffman's post-mortem was headed:

DEFENCE AND LINE NEEDED

Tommy Shields wrote: "we saw Tunney as a capable goalie and two or three forwards who would fit into a hockey team. The remainder simply do not measure up. "[the Flyers need] an entire new defence...at least one complete forward line." His account of the game referred to a "sieve like defence."

Viscount Alexander of Tunis, Canada's Governor General, faced off the opening puck. A local wit volunteered that was as close the Flyers would get to the puck for the rest of the evening.

McGill scored one goal in the first period, four in the second and two in the third.

## BARBARA ANN SCOTT Thrills Big Crowd
## 6,500 FANS

### Ottawa Journal

Figure skating champion, Barbara Ann Scott, thrilled the packed house with a dazzling exhibition between the first and second periods. Her coach, Sheldon Galbraith, gave a flawless demonstration between the second and third periods.

The Flyers looked so bad on ice that one wag cracked: "they should have put Barbara Ann and Sheldon in Flyers' sweaters and given them sticks."

When the Flyers dropped their second exhibition game 6-2 to Coach Bill Cowley's Ottawa senior team the media fixed bayonets.

Only Andy Gilpin and "Red" Gravelle managed to put a puck in the net for the Flyers.

The Flyers' next game was played behind closed doors. There were no spectators.

They defeated the RCAF entry in the Ottawa District Senior League 4-0.

The waves of hopefuls continued:
Flight Lieutenant Bill Macleod
Steve Chmara
AC1 Arthur Schultz
AC1 Arnold Metson
LAC Al Berrigan

Coach Boucher cut eight players and added LAC Johnny Rhude, LAC Bill Grady and Corporal Doug Lyon.

Then he added seven more: Buck Buchanan,

Ross Waugh, Chuck Rafuse, Gus Baudais, Al Lavery, George Wilson, Larry Paget

Boucher's lineup on November 19 had Jack Seymour, Louis Lecompte, Stan Molinski and Jack Maitland on defence.

His forwards were "Red" Gravelle, Len Beatch, Irving Taylor, Hubie Brooks, Tommy Moore, Andy Gilpin, Roy Forbes, Patsy Guzzo and Dick Thomas.

His goaltenders were Ross King and Trev Williams.

Then, he added goaltender Dick Ball from the University of Toronto and cut goaltenders Joe Tunney and Trev Williams. Defensemen Jack Maitland and Jack Seymour were the next to go.

But, the Flyers were in deep trouble. They still didn't have the horses. So, "Sandy" Watson recalls: "we contacted Walter Brown of the Boston Bruins, Jack Adams of Detroit Red Wings, Frank Selke of the Canadiens, Frank Boucher of New York Rangers and Conn Smythe of Toronto Maple Leafs. Only Conn Smythe ignored our distress signal. Frank Selke recommended Andre Laperriere, a steady defenceman with University of Montreal and the consensus among the others was that we should go after George Mara and Wally Halder, the two most talented senior players in North America outside the NHL.

"Then, we put our heads together – Frank and George "Buck" Boucher, Dave MacKell, George Dudley and Norm Dawe from the CAHA, Cece Duncan from the Ottawa District Hockey Association and Jim McCaffrey from the Senators. We agreed to go after five players from the Burghs. We picked up Ab Renaud, Reg Schroeter, Frank Dunster, Pete

Leichnitz and Ted Hibberd."

Renaud, Schroeter and Hibberd formed the highest scoring line in the Ottawa Senior League. The week before they were invited to join the Flyers, they combined to score 12 goals in one game.

Canadian Amateur Hockey Association First Vice President Norm Dawe found himself caught up in the eye of a hurricane. At a CAHA meeting in Quebec City, he placed himself on the record as suggesting Canada send a strong college team to the Olympics.

Dawe watched the Flyers' humiliating 6-2 loss to Bill Cowley's Ottawa Army team as a guest of Wilf Curtis, Chief of the Air Staff.

He attended the two-hour meeting with the Ottawa "Brains Trust" to discuss strengthening the Flyers. His words came back to haunt him and he was forced to issue a press release on December 17 pledging his 100 percent support of the Flyers.

Dawe said that the RCAF Flyers would retain their identity as Canada's Olympic team and that it had been agreed the team needed strengthening. He pledged the CAHA's help.

He said the players would not be playing just for the RCAF or the CAHA. They would be playing for Canada.

Dawe hinted that perhaps strengthening the team might require replacing the entire four-man defence and adding a complete new forward line.

In his press release, he said he wanted it "clearly understood" he was "solidly behind the RCAF" and that Montreal newspaper stories in which he suggested Canada be represented by a college team were "far off the track."

Overnight, eight players were cut to make

room for the newcomers.

To this day, some RCAF players who tried out for the team and who were cut still feed smoldering grudges.

During tryouts, some players who outranked Sergeant/Coach Frank Boucher "tried to pull rank on me. That's where "Sandy" came in handy. He was a Squadron Leader and he outranked them all. They even tried to undercut 'Sandy'. One of them said to me: 'You know, 'Sandy' has an ulcer and he won't be up to snuff to do the manager's job. I'm healthy and I know I can do the job'."

"Sandy" Watson's problems were far from over. George Mara, Wally Halder and Dick Ball had violent reactions to their inoculation shots. They went home to Toronto to recuperate.

Then, a section of the main roof caved in. Dick Ball went for his routine RCAF medical and failed. An X-Ray showed a spot on his lung. The Flyers were without a starting goaltender.

An unknown, Murray Dowey, was recruited at the last minute.

The team was preparing to leave for Europe.

The Ottawa Journal wrote:

"We would wager that Squadron Leader Watson was a happy man when the train moved out and he could feel that he was free from the many irritating circumstances that attended his efforts in recent weeks." (January 9, 1948)

Eighteen players were in Frank Boucher's lineup when the Flyers lost 7-0 to McGill. Ten players would be cut. Only eight of the Opening Night players would be on the boat to England. Only four of the eight – "Red" Gravelle, Patsy Guzzo, Irving Taylor and Louis Lecompte - would see ice time in the eight Olympic matches.

Guzzo and Lecompte played all eight games. Gravelle played seven games and Irving Taylor was used for one game.

The remaining five – Hubie Brooks, Pete Leichnitz, Ross King, Roy Forbes and Andy Gilpin – were the Flyers' "Black Aces" and played only in the team's European exhibition games.

## PACKING FOR EUROPE

Every team member was given a list of things to pack for their three-months tour of Europe:

1. Kitbag
2. Suitcase
3. RCAF greatcoat
4. Civilian greatcoat
5. Civilian hat
6. RCAF cap
7. RCAF uniform
8. Lounge suit
9. Light trousers
10. One pair of boots
11. One pair of shoes
12. One pair of overshoes
13. One pair of slippers
14. Four RCAF shirts
15. Four civilian shirts
16. Ties (civilian and RCAF)
17. Underwear (suggested two suits, four undershirts and shorts)
18. Sweater (heavyweight)
19. Gloves (RCAF and civilian)
20. Socks (suggested six pairs civilian and four

pairs RCAF)
21. Pyjamas (suggested two pairs flannelette)
22. Dressing gown
23. Scarf (one woolen and one silk)
24. Handkerchiefs (suggested dozen white and a half-dozen RCAF)
25. Belt
26. Braces
27. Parka
28. Flying boots (issued)
29. Blazer
30. Shoe polish (to be shared by several members)
31. Button polish (to be shared by several members)

"As soap is on ration in many European countries, members must bring at least six bars apiece. Towels are frequently not provided in European hotels at present. Each member should bring at least two towels. Many such hotels are not equipped for electric razors, hence it is advised to bring a safety razor and blades."


## GETTING OUT OF TOWN

In the 1940s, Ottawa was really a large village. Actually, it was a collection of neighborhoods, small, self-contained wards such as Westboro, Sandy Hill, Lower Town, Lebreton Flats, New Edinburgh and Ottawa East.

Local sportswriters were gentle with their hometown athletes because, most days, they walked among them and knew most of them on a first-name basis.

Before the Flyers left Ottawa by train for

New York, the kindest thing written about them came from the typewriter of Ottawa Journal sportswriter, the late Eddie MacCabe. He wrote that the Flyers were "lightly regarded."

The Ottawa Journal's Bill Westwick wrote "RCAF hopes weren't considered bright" and his colleague, Tommy Shields, allowed, "few conceded them any chance".

Other, out-of-town newspapers raked them unmercifully: "...too small." "...too slow." "...too inexperienced to deal with the onrushing Czechs, Swiss and Swedes."

Universally, the RCAF Flyers were regarded as low flyers.

On December 19, 1947, the Ottawa Citizen allowed "...local sportswriters agree the Olympic team didn't look like world beaters" after they defeated Belleville Intermediates 8-4 in Belleville.

Canada Press writer Jack Sullivan wrote "the Canadian team has not been given much of a chance against strong teams from Switzerland, Czechoslovakia and Sweden."

After the Flyers' 7-0 loss to McGill in their first exhibition game, the Ottawa Journal wrote that "{McGill} threw a bombshell into the entire Olympic hockey scene". Some observers wanted Canada to withdraw completely from the Olympics. Still others wanted the Flyers replaced with a strong university team.

When the Flyers lost their second exhibition game 6-2 to the Bill Cowley coached Ottawa Army team, even the friendly local sportswriters began looking around for over-ripe tomatoes.

A December 18, 1947, editorial in the Ottawa Journal urged the Canadian Amateur Hockey Association to "send a worthy aggregation to St.

Moritz or none at all. Two truly amateur teams – University of Toronto or McGill – would make creditable showings at St. Moritz".

The editorial speculated that the Flyers were "outclassed [appear to be] by those [teams] of every other competing country".

From off-shore, Czech national team coach, expatriate Canadian, Mike Buchna, chimed in to say the Flyers would "lose by perhaps three goals to a top-class Canadian senior club."

The Eastern Bloc's propaganda machine was cranked up to warp speed and branded the RCAF team as professionals masquerading in pilots' uniforms. The Cold War was underway.

The unkindest cut of all came when the coach of Calgary Junior Buffalos of the Southern Alberta Junior League threw down a best-of-three challenge to the Flyers. The winner would represent Canada at St. Moritz. The Flyers and the Canadian Amateur Hockey Association ignored the insult.

When the team was preparing to entrain for New York, they were met by stinging prose from an Ottawa sportswriter who wrote they were "like Arabs folding their tents and sneaking off into the night."

"Sandy" Watson recalls that "when the Chief of the Air Staff, Wilf Curtis, read that he hit the roof.

"Every airman who could walk, every plane that could fly, every bandsman who could play a note was ordered to march down Elgin Street to Union Station to see the team off. RCAF brass was out in force".

The RCAF Central Band belted out the Air Force March Past.

## STATION JAMMED WITH WELL-WISHERS
(Head on Ottawa Citizen story by Jack Koffman)

Air Commodore Dave MacKell, a prominent Ottawa athlete himself, told the well-wishers that the "RCAF was solidly behind the team from the start to the finish."

Coach Frank Boucher told the crowd: "We've got a sound club. The boys will scrap and I believe we have a good chance of winning it all at St. Moritz. Any team that beats us will have to show both hockey class and plenty of fight, of that I'm sure."

The coach's father, George "Buck" Boucher, told the assembled: "They may surprise a few people yet. We have got hold of two good men in Wally Halder and George Mara. They aren't in top shape at present, but they'll come around. The remainder of the boys all look good and I expect them all to play well".

Before the team boarded the Queen Elizabeth in New York, Coach Boucher told reporters he thought the United States team would be the team to beat.

## US IS TEAM TO BEAT
## SAYS RCAF COACH IN N.Y.
Ottawa Journal
January 9, 1948

Coach Boucher told reporters he was "amazed that we finally did make it" on board because of the possibility Canada might not be represented at the Olympics.

When the liner docked at Southampton, he said, "we've got a good club – despite what you may have heard – and we shall do all right."

"Sandy" Watson grinned when he was told British newspapers had nicknamed the Flyers "Canada's mystery team."

"That's just fine; let's keep 'em guessing. We aren't just sure what we're up against either. Most of the other Olympic teams are dark horses, just like us."

Coach Boucher and Manager Watson may have been whistling past the graveyard as they continued to look at the Olympics through rose-coloured glasses. Most serious hockey observers did not concede them any chance of finishing in the medals at St. Moritz.

The jockeying for Gold, Silver and Bronze would be a toss-up among Sweden, Switzerland and Czechoslovakia. The Czechs were heavy favorites to win Gold.

Canada was relegated to duke it out with the United States and Great Britain for fourth place. Canada could finish as low as sixth. Poland, Austria and Italy were written off totally and would finish the tournament in the cellar.

"Sandy" Watson's low flying Flyers left Ottawa by train before hockey fans could grab them and tar and feather them.

"We were the laughing stock of Canada," remembers "Sandy".

"Years later, in a retrospective newspaper article, Pat MacAdam referred to us as 'the Rodney Dangerfields of Ottawa'."

So far, the Flyers hadn't cost the RCAF a nickel. Northland, Spalding and CCM had ponied up with skates and equipment. The only expenses the RCAF absorbed were rations, quarters and transportation for the tryouts.

The players, with the exception of George Mara and Wally Halder, received basic RCAF pay. The Toronto Transit Commission continued to pay Murray Dowey's salary.

So, the RCAF had a free ride and stood to reap hundreds of thousands of dollars in free publicity and good will.

The Canadian Amateur Hockey Association also went along for a free ride. They paid the Flyers' train fare to New York. Old railway timetables show that a round trip coach fare to New York was $17.20. A one-way lower berth cost $3.50 and an upper $2.60.

The team arrived in New York at 8.00 a.m. They could board their liner, Queen Elizabeth, at 4.00 p.m.

They enjoyed a team breakfast at Winston's restaurant opposite Grand Central Station and then the canny Scot, "Sandy" Watson had a brainstorm.

He was cost conscious even though he knew once they boarded the Queen Elizabeth that "Bunny" Ahearne would be responsible for all their travel, hotels and meals. One of the Flyers quipped "every time 'Sandy' took a dollar bill out of his pocket, the King blinked."

"Sandy" called NBC Broadcasting, introduced himself, said he was the manager of the Canadian Olympic hockey team and asked if NBC was "doing any live radio programs at noon".

The producer was "absolutely delighted" to have the Canadian Olympians in his audience for the "Fred Waring and his Pennsylvanians'" show. He promised "Fred will acknowledge your presence in the audience over the radio."

Then, "Sandy" dropped the other shoe.

"Do you think you could serve them lunch?"

So, the Flyers had a free lunch, compliments of NBC. They would have their dinner on board the Queen Elizabeth.

Burgess Meredith and his new bride, Paulette Goddard, were passengers on the Queen Elizabeth. So, too, were Henry Ford and his new bride and former Olympic swimmer and the movies' Tarzan, Johnny Weissmuller. The Flyers were photographed with the celebrities by still photographers and Pathe News.

Murray Dowey recalls that weeks later his wife saw film footage of the shipboard publicity shots and also footage of some of the Olympic Games. "My wife told the theatre manager who she was and he was delighted to make her a copy of the film. She had it for me when we got back home. I threaded up the projector to screen it and it caught fire."

One day out, the Queen Elizabeth hit heavy seas and many meals were returned to nature. The first day of seasickness, few players made it to breakfast. Some were so ill they were afraid they were going to die. The second day they were afraid they were going to live.

When those Flyers able to stand upright and walk ventured out on deck they had to wear their heavy RCAF parkas. To while away the long days and nights they played the usual shipboard games – shuffleboard, deck tennis and deck hockey – betting the odd dollar or Pound.

The Flyers traveled in steerage – the cheapest possible fare. They dressed in their baggy, woolen Air Force blue.

The U.S. team traveled First Class and strutted about the decks in gray flannels, Blazers with a U.S. Olympic crest and distinctive ties. They looked down their noses at the rough-hewn Canadians and boasted they would run them out of the rink.

The Flyers sneaked into First Class to watch first run movies – The McComber Affair, Bachelor Night and I Wonder Who's Kissing Her Now.

One player caroused through the nights with a female passenger until "Sandy" took him to one side and gave him a Dutch uncle talk. From that moment on, he straightened up and flew straight.

Their liner docked at Southampton and, after a brief tussle, with Her Majesty's Customs they were free to travel to London – 80 miles away.

Bad Luck was a stowaway and crossed the Atlantic with the Flyers. The bus taking them to London from Southampton was rear-ended by a tramcar. Only luggage and kit bags piled at the rear saved the players from serious injuries from flying glass.

Some players were sent flying. Tough leather suitcases were slashed but the players were protected by the piled up luggage at the rear. Hours later, "Sandy" Watson was still picking pieces of glass from his hair and uniform.

When their bus arrived in London there were no surprises. London was London. Timeless! Immutable! Defiant!

All along the route from Southampton, they saw bombed out areas. London was no exception. Scaffolding was the giveaway to bomb damage at St. Paul's Cathedral, Sloane Square tube station,

Burlington Arcade on Piccadilly, Buckingham Place and Soho. There were still partial blackouts because of power shortages and "the ever present London fog."

"Bunny" Ahearne billeted the team at the Crofton Hotel in Kensington. It topped the list of "Sandy" Watson's so-called "flea bags."

The lady who checked them in was wearing a fur coat, hat and gloves. Most rooms had no heat. Those that did were heated by coin operated gas heaters. If the Flyers wanted heat they had to insert coins in a meter.

George Mara and Wally Halder would have no truck or trade with a second-rate, two-bit "flea bag." They booked themselves in at the Dorchester Hotel on Park Lane.

The players congregated in the few hotel rooms with heaters.

Before the Flyers left Ottawa, there was a suggestion by a reporter that they would be taking their own rations with them. The RCAF publicity machine quickly scotched that rumor and said the players would make do with the same food Europeans had to eat. Much of Europe was still under wartime rationing conditions.

The fare at the Crofton was sparse, greasy and unappetizing – pork luncheon meat (canned SPAM), a slice of tomato or lettuce and coffee. Tea was usually unavailable and milk, cream and sugar were not available.

Ab Renaud contracted food poisoning and had to be treated at an RCAF hospital in London. Hubie Brooks and Andy Gilpin were also felled by stomach distress.

Four hours after their arrival in London, the Flyers took to the ice at Streatham for a 75-minute workout. They "positively flew," Frank Boucher recalls. The U.S. team that had crossed the Atlantic on the Queen Elizabeth with the Flyers stayed on to watch the Flyers after their own workout.

The same players who smirked at the Flyers on board ship and said they would beat them by 10 goals no longer sported smiling faces.

"Bunny" Ahearne arranged for free tickets to Wembley Arena for the team. The arena had a glassed in VIP section with tables where fans could dine at tables while watching the game.

Ab Renaud recalls: "'Doc' Watson was with "Bunny" Ahearne and they were both cutting into thick steaks. The rest of us were sitting in the cheap seats 'Bunny" had provided for us and we were still trying to digest the swill we had for our dinner."

The Pound Sterling was still one of the strongest convertible currencies in the world. Once worth over $5.00 it had been devalued by 30 percent by Labor Chancellor of the Exchequer, Stafford Cripps.

Ten Pence would still buy a pint of best bitter. Cheap tickets in "the gods" at a West End theatre, according to "Sandy" Watson, were "two and six" – two Shillings and sixpence – about 50 cents.

"Sandy" Watson remembers: "You could have a pint, a feed of fish and chips, take the Tube, see a West End play and still have lots of change left over from a one-Pound note."

"Sandy" enjoyed wholesome food. In Paris, when a maitre d' tried to serve him horsemeat, Ab Renaud recalls, "he almost threw a fit." Then, when the chef substituted eggs he refused to eat them because he was convinced they were ducks' eggs.

George Mara renewed his friendship with the Martell brandy family. In 1939, traveling in France with his father, he met the elder Martell who was killed later fighting with the Resistance in World War Two. Over the years, Mara kept up his friendship with the son and heir of the Martell dynasty.

George's connections and his educated palate served the Flyers well. In Paris, Charles de Gaulle's brother was Mayor.

He received the team at a champagne reception. George told his teammates the wine was plonk – "definitely not the best champagne."

In restaurants across Europe, "Sandy" constantly fretted.

He was always worried he "wouldn't have enough money for tips." He need not have worried. His constant companion was a leather briefcase. It contained $6,000.

When the Flyers played the exhibition game against McGill, Tommy Gorman promised "Sandy" a cut of the box office if he could get World Figure skating champion, Barbara Ann Scott, to skate between periods.

"Sandy" arranged for her and her coach, Sheldon Galbraith, to skate exhibitions.

True to his word, Tommy Gorman gave "Sandy" $6,000.

Fifty years later, I spoke with Barbara Ann Scott King who now lives in Amelia Island, Florida.

"You must be doubly proud of 1948. You won a Gold Medal and, more than any other one person, you were responsible for the hockey team winning their Gold".

"What do you mean?"

"You grubstaked the team. The $6,000 Tommy Gorman gave the team was their mad money."

"What $6,000? What mad money?"

It was the first she had heard of the agreement between Tommy Gorman and "Sandy" Watson.

"I didn't know anything about it. My mother, Mary, (her manager) must have arranged it."

"Sandy's" briefcase was the responsibility of the entire team. He issued orders that it must be with him at all times and players "were to make sure he didn't forget it anywhere". One night he did walk out of a restaurant without it but alert players walked over to the table, retrieved it and chased him down the street.

The Flyers barnstormed throughout Europe until the end of March. Defence Minister Brooke Claxton ordered them home in mid-March:

"It is our desire to get them home while people still remember they are Olympic hockey champions."

For the first time, the Flyers disobeyed orders. They had commitments to fulfill – exhibition games scheduled – and they were broke. They were still singing for their suppers and they couldn't have come home even if they wanted to...

## BARNSTORMING BEFORE THE GAMES
RCAF FLYERS 5 / STREATHAM 5
January 18, 1948

The Flyers were off the boat only 24 hours when they took to the ice for their first exhibition game against Streatham, one of the strongest teams in the English League.

The top British team was stocked with Canadians who remained in England after the war.

The game ended in a 5-5 tie.

The Flyers got off to a fast start. Ted Hibbard and Wally Halder scored in the first period and Flyers were up by a score of 2-0.

Louis Lecompte was serving a minor penalty when George Drysdale, Toronto, and British born Chuck Turner tied the score.

Halder sent Flyers ahead 3-2 midway through the second period but Bud MacEachran of Charlottetown, P.E.I. scored twice within 30 seconds. "Red" Gravelle tied the game, beating Streatham goaltender Montie Reynolds, Windsor, Ontario, with a low, hard shot. Less than 30 seconds later,

Gravelle scored again to put Flyers ahead 5-4. Bud MacEachran completed his hat trick at 14.10 of the third period and that's how the game ended.

Coach Frank Boucher was pleased. The Flyers looked good against tough competition and he knew that with conditioning they would look very good.

Canadian Press reported that "failure to capitalize on numerous opportunities when the opposition was short-handed cost the Flyers victory in their first exhibition game.

The Flyers faded in the final half of the third period and a miscue allowed MacEachran to score the tying goal."

Coach Frank Boucher said after the game: "It was only a fair show and we'll do better when we shake off our sea legs."

## JANUARY 19, 1948

RCAF FLYERS 7          BRIGHTON  6

The newspapers back in Ottawa trumpeted the Flyers' 7-6 triumph over the strong Brighton Tigers. Two weeks earlier, the Tigers had defeated the Czech national team, favourites to win a Gold Medal at St. Moritz.

The Ottawa Journal's sports page headlined:

**CANADIAN OLYMPIC TEAM
DEFEATS   BRIGHTON
TED HIBBERD PLAYS STAR GAME
AGAINST STRONG BRITISH TEAM**

Ted Hibberd and George Mara both scored a pair of goals for the Flyers. Wally Halder, Ab Renaud and Reg Schroeter potted singles. Ted Hibberd slapped home the winning goal in the last seconds of the game.

It was a seesaw battle all night before 10,000 fans.

Lorne Trottier of Ottawa set up Jimmy Chappel for Brighton's first goal of the game. Bobby Lee made it 2-0 but goals by Ted Hibberd and George Mara evened the score. Ab Renaud sent the Flyers ahead 3-2 and Casey Stangle of Montreal tied it up at 3-3.

Halder and Reg Schroeter gave Ottawa a 5-3 lead but Brighton's Lorne Trottier cut the lead to one goal with an unassisted goal with three minutes remaining in the second period.

Chappel, on a pass from Tom Durling, North Battleford, Saskatchewan, tied the game and Gordie Poirier, Maple Creek, Saskatchewan sent Brighton ahead 6-5.

George Mara tied the game halfway through the third period and Ted Hibberd banged in the winner with just seconds remaining.

The Flyers left London for Paris in style. They flew.

## PARIS: JANUARY 21, 1948
LE CLUB DE RACING DE PARIS 5
RCAF FLYERS 3

Flyers faced off against the strongest club team in all of Europe – Le Club de Racing de Paris – before 15,000 fans. The Paris team was riding a 16-game winning streak.

Flyers were off to a fast start with goals from Wally Halder, Ab Renaud and Reg Schroeter and led 3-0 until they ran out of gas.

The Paris Racing Club was a packed team of exceptional Canadian senior players – among them "Mush" Morehouse, Mannie MacIntyre, Pete Bessone, Ossie Carnegie, goaltender Paul Lessard from Hull and New England star Eugene Robert.

A Canadian Press story reported Paris Racing Club carried "a couple of French boys who have trouble getting from one end of the rink to the other without falling down and consequently are rarely used – except when Le Racing is about eight goals in front."

Morehouse scored three goals and MacIntyre and Robert one each.

Flyer Ab Renaud was clipped with a high stick and cut over his eye. "Sandy" Watson and George McFaul sutured him at the bench and Ab was back on the ice for his regular shift.

"If you look closely at the photograph of Reg Schroeter and me with Barbara Ann Scott on our shoulders, you can clearly see the marks of the five stitches over my eye."

A Canadian Press account of the game reported: "a 'bonehead' play by the Flyers gave the Paris team its first goal when the puck was cleared from a corner onto the stick of MacIntyre who was parked alone about 10 feet in front of the nets. Goalie Murray Dowey of Toronto was helpless against the low, cross-fire shot to the far corner."

Flyers gave up another goal on another 'bonehead' defensive slip.

Back home, Canadian crepe hangers moaned about the loss and saw it as an omen of things to come in Olympic competition.

The following morning the team was flown to Zurich on a twin-engine Viking aircraft. An RCAF Dakota carrying "Sandy" Watson and George McFaul and all the team's equipment was close behind.

### TUNING UP IN SWITZERLAND

ZURICH
JANUARY 23
RCAF FLYERS 6
SWISS NATIONAL TEAM 3

Ab Renaud led the Flyers' attack with a pair of goals as Flyers dropped the Swiss national team 6-3 in an exhibition game in Zurich. Patsy Guzzo, Ted Hibberd, Wally Halder and George Mara contributed singles.

The game was played in the antiquated Dolder ice rink before 15,000 fans. Spectators hung from trees or viewed the game from the roofs of buildings.

"Sandy" Watson remembers fans standing in a steady drizzle throughout the game, holding newspapers and umbrellas over their heads. "Nobody in the crowd of 15,000 left".

At game's end there was an inch and a half of water on the ice surface.

The players from both teams were drenched and the Flyers were feeling the effects of playing at an altitude of 6,000 feet.

Until they became accustomed to high altitude their lips turned blue and their breath came in gasps.

After the game, team manager and doctor, "Sandy" Watson prescribed hot baths and compulsory shots of cognac for every Flyer. The cognac was courtesy of George Mara. He had put the touch on one of his family firm's suppliers and was given two cases of the finest procurable.

BASEL
JANUARY 25
BASEL   8  /  RCAF FLYERS 5

The Flyers went down to an 8-5 defeat at the hands of the Swiss national team before 16,000 spectators.

After the loss in Basel, Coach Frank Boucher told reporters: "we don't feel so well now. A couple of the boys have colds after Friday night when we played in the rain and a couple of others are feeling the high, 6,000-feet above-sea-level altitude".

The boards around the outdoor rink were only 10 inches high. Pucks shot over the boards were often lost in snow banks. The Flyers, a team accustomed to using the boards to advantage, banking pucks off them, had to adjust to playing hockey on a figure skating patch.

It would be the only game the Flyers would lose to a national team in their 42-game European tour.

Ab Renaud scored two goals. Patsy Guzzo, George Mara and Wally Halder each scored once.

DAVOS
JANUARY 27
RCAF FLYERS    10 / DAVOS    3

The game was played before a sell-out crowd of 5,000 fans. Schools were closed and fans from neighboring towns flocked to the open-air rink.

The Davos squad was strengthened by the addition of seven members of the Swiss national team.

Wally Halder scored a hat trick. Irving Taylor contributed two goals and three assists. Patsy Guzzo scored twice and singles came off the sticks of Ted Hibberd, Reg Schroeter and Ab Renaud.

The exhibition games were over. The Flyers' tune-ups had ended. The Olympic Games were next.

The Flyers left Davos for St. Moritz on January 28. "Sandy" Watson and Frank Boucher sensed that the team was "jelling."

All the games were played under primitive conditions.

There were no dressing rooms. Players suited up at their hotel and walked to the rink.

The Flyers' game with the United States was postponed because the ice surface was covered with water.

The Europeans were not ready for the Canadian style of "dirty" play. Body contact was not part of the European game. On the other hand, Canadians were not accustomed to the more subtle holding, hooking and "dives" and the not too subtle European habit of "spearing."

Switzerland's winters included the "Fohn", a warm wind not unlike a Canadian Chinook, which would sweep in for a day or two and turn hockey rinks into slush. There was a four-day "Fohn" at the beginning of the tournament but, eventually, weather turned colder.

However, some games had to be played at 7.00 a.m. before the morning sun melted the ice. Some games were played in raging snowstorms. Players had to stop play every ten minutes to clean off the ice.

Wally Halder said "some of the games we played were staged on ice that couldn't possibly have been worse."

## BUNNY AHEARNE vs. AVERY BRUNDAGE

The Flyers settled down in the quiet Swiss resort and spa town of St. Moritz. There were no crowds of tourists to cope with because currency exchange restrictions were in force throughout Europe. The amount of money a person could take out of his country was strictly policed. Tourism was cut back drastically.

The Flyers were immediately confronted with a firestorm that threatened to derail the entire hockey tournament. "Sandy" Watson found himself in the middle of a hornet's nest that saw International Ice Hockey Federation strongman "Bunny" Ahearne and

International Olympic Committee President Avery Brundage locked in a to-the-death combat.

A showdown over which of two American teams would represent the United States very nearly ground the 1948 Olympic Games to a halt.

At issue were claims by two teams claiming to represent the United States - the Amateur Athletic Union or the U.S. Amateur Hockey Association. Both teams claimed to be the official U.S. team.

The Amateur Athletic Union traveled to Europe in style.

They flew on American Overseas Airlines. The upstart Amateur Hockey Association team sailed on the Queen Elizabeth with the RCAF Flyers.

The Americans, wearing Blazers and flannels, traveled First Class; the Flyers were below decks in Steerage.

"Sandy" Watson recalls the tinderbox situation had the potential to be "the greatest political hockey catastrophe of the century."

At a 1947 meeting of the International Ice Hockey Federation in Prague, the Amateur Hockey Association replaced the Amateur Athletic Union and was recognized as the United States' member of the International Ice Hockey Federation. The vote was 9-2.

The IIHF and the Swiss Olympics organizing committee recognized the A.H.A. entry.

The A.A.U. was deemed to be ineligible because it had been replaced by the A.H.A. as the governing body in the U.S.

Avery Brundage, a former U.S. decathlon Olympian, was an American Olympic Committee Member from 1936 to 1973 and International Olympic Committee President from 1952 to 1972.

Early in his mandates, he was seen as the guardian of the Olympic flame of the pure amateur in Olympic competition. Towards the end, his hard line position painted him in a corner as a dinosaur and a social snob.

Being an Olympian carried an aura of snobbery and social standing. The great American sculler, John Kelly, Princess Grace's father, was denied entry to the Henley Regatta in England because he was a bricklayer and, therefore, had an unfair advantage over "gentlemen."

The A.A.U. hockey team was composed of players from Dartmouth, a small Ivy League college in Hanover, New Hampshire.

Dartmouth dominated U.S. college hockey in the 1940s and between 1941 and 1946 went 46 straight games without a loss.

Dartmouth was knee deep in talent. Their varsity team had 23 lettermen competing for 14 positions plus a promising crop of rookies. Dartmouth had enough talent for two teams – one to compete in the Olympics in St. Moritz and the other to compete in college play back home.

Three Riley brothers starred at Dartmouth. Two went to St. Moritz. Jack played for the A.H.A. team and Joe played for the A.A.U. club. Billy Riley stayed home. He had a wife and two children and his wife put her foot down – he wasn't going to Switzerland for two weeks if he wasn't sure he'd even be playing.

Avery Brundage threw down the gauntlet. He termed the A.H.A. team "an outlaw organization" that was sponsored by commercial interests for moneymaking purposes and "will never be recognized by the United States Olympic Committee or any other amateur organizations in this country."

Officials in charge of the hockey tournament insisted on describing it as an official Olympic event. The International Olympic Committee, on the other hand, said it could not recognize the tournament as part of the Olympics because the International Ice Hockey Federation was the "controlling body" of International Amateur hockey.

Brundage charged that the A.H.A. team was sponsored by arena owners and their hockey rinks housed professional teams. A symbol of Brundage's charges of professionalism was present in the flesh in St. Moritz. Walter Brown, the manager of the A.H.A. team, was the owner of Boston Garden.

Brundage said in Chicago in July, 1947: "There is an important principle at stake – that is, whether any federation shall be permitted to flaunt amateur rules for 47 months out of 48 and then purify itself for one month in order to participate in the Olympic Games so that they may use the prestige of an Olympic competition in furthering its commercial pursuits during the aforesaid 47 months."

IIHF President "Bunny" Ahearne picked up the gauntlet. He threatened, if the A.H.A. entry was vetoed by Brundage's group: "all other IIHF countries, including Canada, would withdraw" from the Olympics.

## HOCKEY CANCELLED
## REMOVED FROM
## OLYMPIC GAMES

So bannered the head on a January 30th, 1948, Canadian Press story datelined St. Moritz.:

St, Moritz – Jan. 30 – (CP) The IOC announced tonight that ice hockey has been cancelled from the fifth winter games, which got under way today, beneath a cloud created by the hockey controversy involving rival factions from the U.S.

Development piled on development. Even faster than the Czechs could score goals, rumours and speculation buzzed about hotel corridors in the playground of millionaires.

As the plot thickened, the Olympic Press Bureau issued a communique asserting that St. Moritz Mayor Karl Nater had advised the Olympic Committee that if the AHA (U.S.) and Swiss hockey teams took to the ice, the police had instructions to bar them.

The release added that the Mayor had asked IOC President Sigfrid Edstrom for a formal order but Edstrom was reluctant to comply because a meeting of the IOC was to be held later.

Because of Edstrom's refusal, the order was never carried out.

Canadian Press staff writer, Jack Sullivan, wrote that same day: "The RCAF Flyers, still in the dark as to whether they are playing for the Olympic, World, or just exhibition honours, came from behind to match the first period goal by the Swedish team and score another in each of the last two periods."

Ahearne went even further. He said all IIHF member teams would go down the road to Davos and stage the World Hockey championships. There would be no Olympic hockey.

The Swiss Olympic organizing committee was in a box. They knew if they allowed the collegian A.A.U. team to play that all other countries would pull out. The Swiss needed the box office receipts.

Then, Brundage pulled another rabbit out of his hat.

If the A.H.A. team was allowed to play he would withdraw the entire U.S. Olympic team – skiers, bobsledders and figure skaters. On January 20, by a vote of 68 to 6, the United States Olympic Committee endorsed Brundage's threat to withdraw ALL American athletes.

The Mayor of St. Moritz said the equivalent of "Nuts." His reaction was: "That's nice!"

The International Olympic Committee solved the problem two days before the Official Opening of the Games.

They kicked both U.S. teams out.

Two hours before the Olympic flame was lit the IOC caved in. The A.H.A. would be allowed to play.

Then, the "catastrophe" began to take on aspects of a comic opera.

The A.H.A. hockey team marched at the Opening. They wore blue coats, hats and fur-lined aviators' boots. To the surprise of all, the A.A.U. team marched, too. They wore white mackinaws and matching hats.

Brundage told the collegians they would be in the official records books as having played – even though they would not play a game.

The International Olympic Committee ruled that if the A.H.A. team took to the ice the hockey tournament would not be recognized as an Olympic event.

"Sandy" Watson was dragged into the backroom farce early one morning.

"I've never told anyone this story before. Coach Frank Boucher and I were sharing a room. At 2.00 a.m. there was a knock on our door and we were both awakened. It was Sidney Dawes, Canada's International Olympic Committee Member. I was in my pajamas and Frank was sitting up in bed.

"Frank was wide awake and heard it all. Dawes told us that Brundage said the A.H.A. should not be allowed to play because they are all pros. The A.A.U. team should be recognized because they were all college students.

"But, 'Bunny' Ahearne had told us that if the A.A.U. played there'd be no Olympics. He'd move hockey to Davos and hold the World's there. Every team would go except the A.A.U. I felt badly. We didn't come this far to play only in the World's. We came to play in the Olympics.

"Dawes said to me, conspiratorially, that we should quit the Canadian Amateur Hockey Association and form a new body. Canada would go into this new grouping with the United States. Dawes said we could break 'Bunny' Ahearne and the IIHF and all the other nations would follow.

"I told Dawes: 'No way. No way I can go for this'. Frank heard every word. We talked until about 4.00 in the morning. All the news was – no Olympics.

"That morning when we went to dress we didn't know if we'd be playing in the World's or the

103

Olympics. Avery Brundage was sweating bullets, ranting for anyone and all to hear that the A.H.A. would not play a game in Europe.

"For the Swiss, hockey meant the most money in gate receipts. If the Olympic and World's were not held in St. Moritz, they'd have to refund a lot of ticket money. I think that was "Bunny" Ahearne's trump card. That's where he won.

"Our opening game was against Sweden and we found out 10 minutes before the opening puck was dropped that the A.H.A. would represent the U.S. Ahearne was absolutely ruthless. He said that no team in the IIHF would ever play the American A.A.U. team and they never played a game.

"For Dawes to come to me and ask me to break with the Canadian Amateur Hockey Association was immorality at its highest pitch.

"I have no idea what was behind Dawes' suggestion that Canada fall in behind the A.A.U. The war was over. He was a businessman and perhaps he saw a better corporate future in Canada and the U.S. by throwing in his lot with the Americans. I've never concerned myself with or understood business politics."

The A.H.A. came forward with some "face-saving" suggestions that fell just short of absurd:

1. If the U.S. did not win a medal then the competition could be considered an Olympic event.
2. If the U.S. did win a medal then the results would not be recognized

In the end, the Americans lost games to Canada, Switzerland and Czechoslovakia and are in the record books ("with an asterisk") in fourth position – out of the medals. The U.S. team thrashed Poland 23-4 and Italy 31-1.

The outclassed team from Italy lost all eight games by scores of 23-0 to Sweden, 21-1 to Canada, 22-3 to Czechoslovakia and 16-0 to Switzerland.

It wasn't until February 7, when teams had seven games under their belts, that the games already played were accorded official recognition by the Olympic poobahs.

Some U.S. Olympians believe that if the two rival American teams had joined and picked one team they could have won the 1948 tournament handily.

The A.A.U. team had to be content with a two-weeks, all expenses paid vacation in St. Moritz.

They were not even allowed practice time on ice surfaces because all the rinks were controlled by the IIHF.

A.H.A. forward Jack Kirrane came back to captain a U.S. team in 1960 and win a Gold Medal in the Squaw Valley, California, Games.

When it was all over and the ice chips had settled the International Olympic Committee gave serious consideration to excluding hockey from all future Olympics.

## THE MOMENT OF TRUTH

Frank Boucher was alone in a St. Moritz hotel room. He was alone with a pencil and notepad – and his thoughts.

Friday, January 30, was Frank Boucher's day of decision – the day he would have to make the gut wrenching decisions who his eleven starting players would be.

"Sandy" Watson decided the team would not march in the Opening Parade the next morning.

The three-hour procession of athletes and the Opening Ceremony would be too tiring.

He wanted his players fresh and rested when they took to the ice against Sweden the next day – if, indeed, the hockey tournament was going to proceed.

"Sandy" instructed Patsy Guzzo to advise George Dudley of his decision. He was over-ruled by Dudley. The Flyers would participate in opening ceremonies.

The team turned out in Air Force blue uniforms.

Barbara Ann Scott marched at the head of the Canadian contingent. Hubie Brooks carried the Canadian flag and George McFaul was up front with a CANADA placard.

The athletes marched five blocks and entered the Stadium where they swore the Olympic Oath.

There was little press coverage of the 1948 Olympics. The only Canadian newsman present was Jack Sullivan of Canadian Press. Television was still in diapers and the only cameramen present were from movie newsreel companies.

Frank Boucher's personal Gethsemane was upon him. He had tough decisions to make.

He had yet to post his starting lineup. He had 17 players and Olympic rules allowed him to dress only eleven plus a backup goaltender. Five players would not dress and would watch the games as spectators.

Some of his lineup was already set in his mind: Murray Dowey would be his starting goaltender and Ross King his backup. Dowey was a stand-up goaltender and he was quick with his trapper glove.

Wally Halder and George Mara were automatics. Both had played themselves into shape since their arrival at the Ottawa Auditorium. Patsy Guzzo and Louis Lecompte were both 33 years old. Would their experience win out over the legs of the younger guns? Louis Lecompte's work clearing the puck was sloppy and suspect. His two mistakes in Paris resulted in a 5-3 loss to the Club de Racing.

Andre Laperriere and Frank Dunster were both solid performers on the blue line. Laperriere was a heady scientific defenceman and Dunster was a hitter. Would Dunster's aggressive play pass muster with European referees?

Ab Renaud and Reg Schroeter were proven goal scorers, tough two-way players who had years of top-drawer senior competition and playoff pressure under their belts.

"Red" Gravelle was only 18 years old and still had much to learn. He was chippy and might take "stupid penalties", retaliating to a hook or a slash. Those were some of the tangibles that Frank had to weigh the night before the Flyers first game against Sweden.

He had only seen the Flyers play as a team in a handful of exhibition games in London, Paris, and Switzerland. In the end, he went with experience.

That morning the United States' A.H.A. team had scored a 5-4 upset victory over Switzerland. Frank finished writing down his starting line-up of eleven players and gave it to Patsy Guzzo to take to George Dudley at his hotel. Patsy didn't know his name was on the list until Trainer George McFaul told him his equipment was ready for the opening game. "The Chosen" knew they would be dressing against Sweden.

107

Frank had the unenviable chore of leaving five names off the list. They would be his "Black Aces" – spares who would not dress but who could be called upon as substitutes in the event of injury or suspension.

Ross King was Murray Dowey's understudy for all eight Olympic games.

Irving Taylor was one of the eleven Chosen Ones for Game One. Either, his play didn't please Coach Boucher or he was still favoring an injured knee. He was dropped from the lineup and replaced in the next seven games by "Red" Gravelle.

Taylor was not the team player Boucher wanted. He tended to hang on to the puck and try to stickhandle through the opposition on solo rushes. He did not pass the puck.

Pete Leichnitz was one of the inexperienced young guns who was just beginning his career in senior hockey. Hubie Brooks just didn't have the hockey skills of his more talented teammates. Roy Forbes and Andy Gilpin were victims of the numbers game. They had the experience and the talent but Frank had no room to maneuver.

As the tournament unfolded, none of the Black Aces, except "Red" Gravelle, dressed for any of games against national teams. It was a bitter pill to swallow.

They had crossed an ocean to play for their country. They were sacrificing three months of their lives to tour Europe with the RCAF Flyers.

They had mixed emotions. How can I accept a Gold Medal when I wasn't on the ice for any of the games? In their eyes, the Gold medals they were awarded were tarnished long before the natural agents of decay – time and corrosion – could begin to diminish their luster.

# GAME ONE
## FLYERS vs SWEDEN
## RCAF FLYERS 3 SWEDEN 1

Let the Games begin!

The Flyers showed their critics they could compete with the very best.

They defeated top ranked Sweden 3-1 in what Canadian Press described as a "tough, bruising contest. Sticks flew and tempers flared in the final minutes of the game with a free-for-all threatening.

"Penalties were handed out freely. The RCAF goalie, Murray Dowey, was waved to the penalty box with eight seconds remaining" for throwing the puck forward, a violation under Olympic rules.

Sweden scored before the first period was three minutes old. Two minutes later, George Mara took a pass from Patsy Guzzo and tied the game.

Mara's goal was probably the biggest goal of the tournament. It noticeably lifted up a team that was given no chance against the Swedes, Czechs, British and Americans. The fired up Flyers skated with newly found confidence. A rag-tag collection of last minute recruits proved to themselves they could play with the world's best veterans.

Wally Halder broke the tie with what turned out to be the winning goal at 2:07 of the second period on a pass from Ab Renaud. Reg Schroeter banged in an insurance goal with an assist from Louis Lecompte at the 35-second mark of the third period.

Some Flyers, Patsy Guzzo among them, saw their Gold Medals vanishing when their marquee player, Wally Halder, was cut down by a vicious, deliberate chop to his head. Halder was down on the ice for what must have seemed to be an eternity. But, he got up, under his own steam, felt the back of his head, shook himself and skated to the bench. He was back on the ice for his next shift.

When the eight-game tournament was over, Flyers were unanimous in branding Sweden as the "dirtiest" team they had played. Wally Halder said: "we never ran into so much slashing and hooking in any league as we did".

After the victory, it was obvious that a group of individuals who had never played together before was fast becoming a disciplined team.

Throughout the tournament, the Flyers took four times as many penalties as any other team in competition.

Some of the rules and calls by referees were laughable. A player could not shoot the puck if he was lying on the ice and was penalized if he did.

George Mara tripped and, as he fell, he shot the puck into the net. The goal was disallowed and Mara was penalized.

A goaltender could not throw the puck forward. Murray Dowey did and was penalized.

## SUMMARY – GAME ONE

First period
1. Sweden – Lindstrom (Nurnala)  2:30
2. Canada  - Mara (Guzzo)             4:35
Penalty – Renaud
Second Period
3.  Canada – Halder (Renaud)        2:07
Penalty – R. Ericson
Third Period
4. Canada – Schroeter (Lecompte)   :35
Penalties – Nurnala (minor and misconduct), Laperriere, Dunster, Dowey

# Flyers Photo Album

An inspiring collection of rare photographs
of on-ice action, ceremonies, artifacts and
memorabilia commemorating a unique time
in hockey history.

Top: The 1948 Flyers marching towards Olympic glory in St. Moritz.
Bottom: An early team photo of the Flyers in Switzerland.

Top: The Flyers' second line of Ab Renaud (left - 4 goals + 10 assists), Ted Hibberd (center - 3 goals, four assists) and Reg Schroeter (right - 12 goals, 5 assists) contributed 19 of the team's 69 goals.
Bottom: St. Mortiz Olympic ID badge.

George Mara, Wally Halder's linemate, scored 17 goals and assisted on nine others. Wally Halder and George Mara were 1-2 in goals and points

Teenage goaltender Murray Dowey was a last-minute substitute. Described as the "second best goalie in the Toronto
area - Turk Broda was the best" -  he recorded five shutouts
and allowed only five goals in eight games.

Wally Halder, with 21 goals and eight assists, led scorers from all teams and was named Most Valuable Player.

Top: Canada versus Sweden in Olympic hockey action at
St. Moritz. The Flyers soon had critics eating their words.
Bottom: High scoring forward Ab Renaud's skates and
sweater on display at the Olympic Hall of Fame in Calgary.

Top: More Olympic action against Sweden. The Canadians were widely praised for their skating and stick-handling abilities - and for their ability to seemingly score at will. Bottom: A flyer's passport, memorabilia from an heroic time in hockey history.

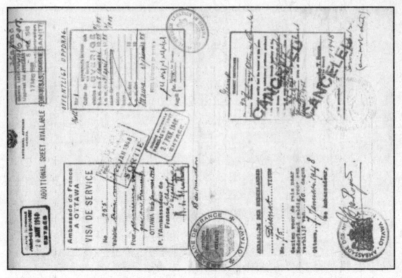

Top: Murray Dowey prepares to smother the puck in the game against Switzerland. The cricket style cap was not part of his normal equipment. He wore it to keep the sun out of his eyes. (photo also appears on book cover)
Bottom: The Flyers' Team passport.

Top: Murray Dowey leans over a player in Olympic hockey action as a crowd in the stands watches with interest. Bottom: Andre Laperriere rounds his own net watched by Flyers goalie Murray Dowey, defenceman Frank Dunster and high scoring forward George Mara.

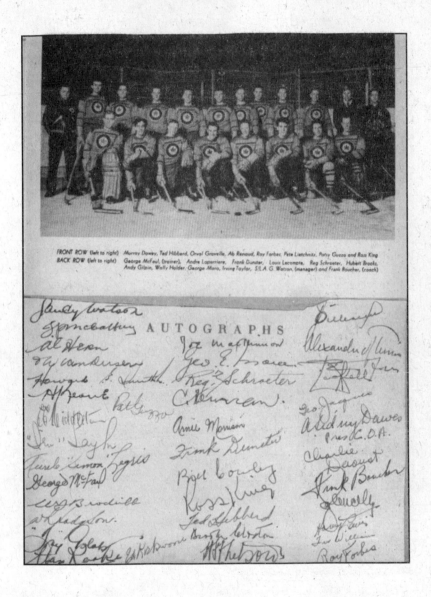

FRONT ROW (left to right)  Murray Dowey, Ted Hibberd, Orval Gravelle, Ab Renaud, Roy Forbes, Pete Listchnitz, Patsy Guzzo and Ross King
BACK ROW (left to right)  George McFaul, (trainer), Andre Laperriere, Frank Dunster, Louis Lecompte, Reg Schroeter, Hubert Brooks,
Andy Gilpin, Wally Halder, George Mara, Irving Taylor, S/L A. G. Watson, (manager) and Frank Boucher, (coach)

Team picture autographed by players. This was in much greater demand at the end of the Olympics than at the start when Canada's team had yet to prove itself.

REATE... ...RFORMANCES TORONTO DAILY STAR Mon., Feb. 16, 1948 3

BARBARA ANN, centre background, stands behind the bride and groom under crossed hockey sticks of winning Canadian Olympic hockey team behind bride and groom

—A.P. Photo

The Toronto Star covered this unusual wedding featuring an archway of raised hockey sticks and the participation of the Canadian Olympic hockey team - the Flyers.

Hubie Brooks married his Danish bride, Birthe Grontved at St. Moritz following the hockey tournament. Barbara Ann Scott was Maid of Honour and "Sandy" Watson was Best Man. Brooks' teammates provided the archway of hockey sticks for the Bride and groom to pass under.

As the above photos demonstrate, the Canadian team grew more enthusiastic with each victory photograph taken. Here the victorious Flyers celebrate after the final whistle, having won the Olympic Games with an outstanding gold medal performance.

Top: Cavalcade of Buick convertibles transport triumphant Flyers to RCAF Headquarters.

Bottom: NHL great George "Buck" Boucher, Chief of the Air Staff Wilf Curtis, Defence Minister Brooke Claxton and Ottawa Mayor Stan Lewis "take the salute" as the Flyers drive past.

## A Message Of Welcome

CANADA

MINISTER OF NATIONAL DEFENCE

Welcome home R.C.A.F. Flyers!
All of Canada and particularly your comrades
in the Armed Forces are proud of the fine
record you made in winning the Olympic Games.
Reports from abroad showed that everywhere
your good sportsmanship and conduct carried
higher the name of Canada.

*Brooke Claxton*

Defence Minister Claxton Sends Greetings To The Champions

Congratulatory letters like the one above poured in from across the country from government and military officials and from businesses and members of the Canadian public.

Top: A Flyers group photo in Ottawa.
Bottom: Squadron Leader "Sandy" Watson, Air Marshal Wilf Curtis, Governor General Alexander, Defence Minister Brooke Claxton and Flyers' Coach Frank Boucher.

Top: Governor General Lord Alexander of Tunis presents a commemorative ring to "Red" Gravelle.
Bottom: A popular post card of the day, featuring Canadian Olympic medalists for skating, including Barbara Ann Scott, and the 1948 Olympic Gold medal-winning Flyers.

Barker's Biscuits of Toronto was exceptionally proud that three of the top Flyers - Murray Dowey, Wally Halder and George Mara - had al played for the Barker's Hockey Club prior to going to the Olympics. Barker's congratulatory ad also plays up Torontro origins of these remarkable players.

A Czech cartoon of the day plays up the gifted Canadian hockey players. The Czechs praised the Canadians and said they had learned much from them.

'1948 Flyers Gold Medalists Ab Renaud (left) and Reg Schroeter (right) hoist fellow Gold Medalist, figure skater Barbara Ann Scott, to their shoulders. That's not a Gold Medal she is biting. It is something more "valuable" - a piece of rare post-war chocolate that Reg passed to her.

Chief of Air Staff examines Roy Forbes' Gold Medal.

Reg Schroeter, Barbara Ann Scott King and Ab Renaud at a reunion at the Calgary Olympics, recreated (and held) the historic photo that had been seen throughout the world.

After the Flyers' impressive Gold Medal performance at the Olympics, Canadians everywhere savoured the taste of victory with a slice of hockey history.

# GAME TWO
## RCAF vs GREAT BRITAIN
## RCAF FLYERS  3    GREAT BRITAIN 0

The British were defending World and Olympic hockey champions. The Flyers knew they would be no pushovers. Defeating Great Britain was as important to the Flyers as winning a Gold Medal.

Canada's cachet as the world's best was besmirched by Great Britain's Gold Medal performance in the 1936 Olympics. Canadians from coast to coast were shocked and stunned. Defeating Great Britain meant restoring national pride and recapturing hockey supremacy.

The stage was set for the showdown but the weatherman did not cooperate. The game was played in a driving snowstorm. By the time the game was over there was an inch of snow on the outdoor ice surface.

Based on a Canadian Press story, the Ottawa Journal headlined:
PENALTIES AND REFEREES A JOKE
IN THREE-HOUR GAME IN SNOW

The Flyers scored a goal a period to defeat Britain. Reg Schroeter converted a pass from Ab Renaud to score the winning goal at 1:08 of the first period. George Mara scored an unassisted goal in the second period and Wally Halder salted the game away with a third period goal.

At times, the players had difficulty seeing the puck in the blizzard.

Canadian Press reporter Jack Sullivan wrote that the "penalty sprinkled struggle" was "delayed considerably by unnecessary whistle blowing" by referees who handed out a total of 21 penalties – "most of them for questionable offences."

"The march to the penalty box was a joke among players of both clubs".

Ab Renaud broke in on the British goaltender in the first period and beat him cleanly with a back-hander. The Swiss goal judge ruled it did not go in. Players on both teams conceded it was a good goal.

Flyers' Manager, "Sandy" Watson protested and the goal judge was replaced. Team Manager Watson said later that the game official refereed an exhibition game in Switzerland and had "robbed" the Flyers of two goals.

The Flyers missed three more goals in the first period when Halder and Renaud both rang pucks off goalposts with the British goaltender out of the net. Later, Renaud "rode in alone" but failed to score when the goaltender slid out and "made a spectacular save".

The game took more than three hours to complete and turned into a farce as the referees took more-or-less 'blind guesses' in their whistle tooting. It was cleanly played throughout despite the 21 penalties and players of both sides laughed and wisecracked when given penalties. The Flyers were assessed 12 penalties and Great Britain nine.

Jack Sullivan wrote: "About 2,000 spectators saw the game, held in an open-air rink, and they cheered and hooted as the march to the penalty box continued at a dizzy rate.

"Late in the game, the ice covered with an inch of snow, it was almost impossible to control the puck. "The contest limped to a close as a swirling snowstorm broke over Olympic Stadium."

## SUMMARY – GAME TWO

First Period
1. Canada – Schroeter (Renaud)     1:08
Penalties – Davey, Schroeter, Baillie, Halder, Guzzo

Second Period
2. Canada – Mara                           3:47
Penalties – Murray, Syme (2), Halder (2), Oxley (2) Guzzo, Lecompte

Third Period
3. Canada – Halder (Lecompte)          16:00
Penalties – A. Green, Guzzo (2), Hibberd, Baker, Dunster (2)

# GAME THREE
## FLYERS vs. POLAND
## FLYERS 15    POLAND 0

The Flyers totally overwhelmed an outclassed Polish team by a score of 15-0. They scored five goals in the first period, six in the second and four in the third.

Wally Halder scored four goals and assisted on two others. Reg Schroeter scored a hat trick and picked up one assist.

Ab Renaud had a pair of goals and a pair of assists and George Mara and "Red" Gravelle both scored twice. Mara also had three assists. Andre Laperriere, Louis Lecompte and Patsy Guzzo had singles.

Between periods, Trainer George McFaul served tea and lemons to the players on both teams. During play, the Polish goaltender suffered a cut nose. Dr. "Sandy" Watson and George McFaul stitched him up at the Flyers' bench.

Only three penalties were called in a cleanly played game. Chivalry was alive and well. When a player was down on the ice he was helped up by an opposing player.

Earlier in the day, soft ice forced postponement of the scheduled game between Switzerland and Great Britain.

## SUMMARY – GAME THREE

First Period
1. Canada – Renaud (Halder)    1:55
2. Canada -  Lecompte          10:50
3. Canada -  Schroeter (Halder) 12:21
4. Canada – Schroeter (Halder) 15:16
5. Canada -  Gravelle (Guzzo)   19:21
Penalty – Renaud
Second Period
6. Canada – Renaud             2:40
7. Canada – Guzzo (Mara)       4:03
8. Canada -  Halder (Schroeter) 6:30
9. Canada -  Halder            7:50
10.Canada - Mara – (Guzzo)                7:54
11. Canada – Schroeter (Renaud) 16:32
Penalties – None
Third Period
12. Canada – Halder (Renaud)    4:03
13. Canada -  Gravelle (Mara)   11:11
14. Canada -Laperriere (Mara)   14:26
15. Canada – Mara (Guzzo)       15:50
Penalties – Kolasa, Laperriere

# GAME FOUR
## FLYERS vs ITALY
## FLYERS 21    ITALY 1

The Flyers rolled to their fourth straight victory crushing a pathetic Italian squad 21-1.

Italy scored its only goal on a fluke at 8:00 of the third period. Flyers' goaltender, Murray Dowey's scoreless streak was broken at 225 minutes and 30 seconds. He had not been scored on since Sweden scored in the first three minutes of their opening game.

Every Flyer except Murray Dowey figured in scoring in the 21-1 triumph.

Canadian Press writer Jack Sullivan filed this report: "the blond youngster from Toronto might have had another shutout except for a fluke goal scored against him in the third period of Canada's 21-1 victory over Italy."

George Mara had five goals and five assists.

Wally Halder also had a turkey shoot - scoring five goals and assisting on another.

Patsy Guzzo and Ted Hibberd contributed hat tricks. Reg Schroeter scored twice. Ab Renaud had a goal and four assists.

The Italian team did not have a single shot on the Canadian goal. Their lone goal was scored from behind the Canadian net.

Murray Dowey's complacency and lapse in concentration cost him a shutout. He was slow sliding his skate against the goal post and it resulted in an Italian goal.

Canadian Press writer Jack Sullivan reported: "Despite Canada's excellent record, observers still consider Czechoslovakia the team to beat."

Italian newspapers did not take kindly to a 21-1 humiliation at the hands of Canada. They nicknamed aggressive Canadian forward, Wally Halder, "The Brute."

Wally "The Brute" Halder was only penalized once during all the years he played with University of Toronto.

Seeing "Sandy" Watson stitch up cuts at the bench, they nicknamed him "The Butcher". Perhaps, they were unaware he was a medical doctor.

There were only 75 spectators in the stands for the Canada-Italy game.

### SUMMARY – GAME FOUR
### RCAF FLYERS vs ITALY

First Period

| | |
|---|---|
| 1. Canada – Halder (Lecompte) | :45 |
| 2. Canada - Dunster | 3:12 |
| 3. Canada – Hibberd | 4:02 |
| 4. Canada - Mara | 5:48 |
| 5. Canada – Mara (Hibberd) | 6:01 |
| 6. Canada - Schroeter (Halder,Renaud) | 6:50 |
| 7. Canada – Halder (Renaud) | 7:00 |
| 8. Canada - Mara | 9:00 |
| 9. Canada – Halder (Renaud) | 14:52 |
| 10. Canada - Guzzo (Mara) | 16:40 |
| 11. Canada – Hibbard (Mara) | 17:12 |

Penalty – Laperriere

Second Period

| | |
|---|---|
| 12. Canada – Hibbard (Mara) | 2:13 |
| 13. Canada – Renaud (Schroeter) | 6:14 |
| 14. Canada – Mara | |

7:00
15.      Canada      –      Halder      (Laperriere)
12:00
16.      Canada      –      Schroeter      (Renaud)
16:00
17.      Canada      –      Gravelle      (Mara)
19:00
Penalty – Laperriere

Third Period

18.          Canada          –          Halder
10
19.          Canada          –          Guzzo
2:00
20.          Italy          –          Menardi
8:00
21.      Canada      –      Guzzo      (Mara)
9:00
22.          Canada          –          Mara
12:00
Penalty - Laperriere

# GAME FIVE
## FLYERS vs.U.S.A.
### RCAF FLYERS    12    U.S.A.   3

Frank Boucher considered the U.S. team the team to beat.

The two teams could not have asked for a better stage for their showdown. It was a cold, crisp winter morning. The ice surface was perfect and the Flyers seized the day. With their newly found confidence and ideal conditions, they positively flew.

The American team crossed the Atlantic with the Flyers on the Queen Elizabeth. They were nattily attired in crested Blazers and gray flannels.

In sharp contrast, the Flyers wore baggy air force wool. The Americans traveled First Class. The Flyers traveled steerage.

They met on deck when newsreel and still photographers asked them to pose. The Americans strutted and boasted they would beat the Canadians by 10 goals.

When the teams took to the ice, Wally Halder was smarting from their insults. He scored six goals and assisted on one.

George Mara scored four and Louis Lecompte and Reg Schroeter scored the remaining two goals.

The game was only 30 seconds old when Wally Halder rifled a hard wrist shot past the U.S. netminder.

It was the worst defeat ever for a U.S. Olympic team.

Canadian Press reported Wally Halder scored six goals – "four of them scored in brilliant solo efforts."

Halder scored 30 seconds after the opening face-off with a waist-high shot from 35 feet out that caught the U.S. goaltender completely off guard.

The Flyers poured it on in the second period scoring four goals within six minutes.

Halder scored two in slightly more than a minute. Flyers led 7-1 after two periods. At one point in the third period, the Flyers were ahead 9-2.

Before the game, the Flyers had doubting Thomases in the press: "…expert opinion here has been that the Flyers were one of the less powerful teams Canada has sent over. The Czech squad, on the other hand, has been rated highly. Its Number One star is Jaroslav Drobny, who doubles as a Davis Cup tennis star".

After Canada drubbed the U.S. 12-3, the worm began to turn. Reporters began to sit up and take notice. One conceded: "Now things look different. The five straight victories rolled up by Canada and the ease of their victory today make it look as though the Canadians are no set-ups after all. They appear to be Czechoslovakia's main threat – since the third undefeated club – Switzerland – barely beat the United States 5-4."

## SUMMARY – GAME FIVE

First Period
1. Canada – Halder                                    :30
2. Canada - Mara (Hibberd)                      6:30
3. U.S. – Cunliffe (Mather)                       14:45
4. Canada – Halder (Schroeter, Renaud)   19:50
Penalties – Lecompte, Halder, Mara

Second Period
5. Canada – Halder (Renaud, Schroeter)       :30

6.  Canada -  Lecompte (Hibberd)          2:00
7.  Canada -  Mara                             4:00
8.  Canada – Halder                            5:40
Penalties – Lecompte (2), Renaud, Riley

Third Period
9.           U.S.           -              Priddy
:20
10.          Canada          –          Halder
2:00
11.       Canada          -          Halder
3:10
12.          U.S.           –          Cunliffe
4:30
13.       Canada      –      Schroeter     (Halder)
12.:30
14.       Canada      –      Mara      (Hibberd)
13:40
15. Canada – Mara (Guzzo)
Penalties – Lecompte, Riley

# GAME SIX
## FLYERS VS. CZECHOSLOVAKIA
## RCAF FLYERS 0    CZECHOSLOVAKIA  0

Game conditions were ideal. The ice surface was perfect.

This was the game that would separate the men from the boys. The winner would probably go home with the Gold Medals. But, the battle of the titans failed to provide a clear-cut winner.

The teams battled to a scoreless tie.

Meanwhile, Switzerland took over first place in standings with six consecutive wins. But, they had yet to play the Flyers or the Czechs.

Flyers were still ahead in goals for and against. In six games they scored 54 goals and gave up only five. They would be the last five goals scored on Murray Dowey.

George Mara had the best scoring opportunity for the Flyers. Midway through the second period he rifled a bullet from 15-feet out. It was aimed at the right-hander corner but Czech goaltender, Bohumil Modry, managed to deflect it.

Flyers peppered Modry with eight shots in three minutes but could not penetrate his armor.

Czechoslovakia's best chance came when Jaroslav Drobny golfed a shot from the blueline, which almost got past Dowey. The rebound came out five feet and four Czech players pounced on it. Dowey made three quick saves and four of his teammates bunched up in the crease to hold the fort.

George Mara was sent off for interference and Czech coach Mike Buchna sent five forwards against the Flyers. Defencemen Louis Lecompte and Frank Dunster reached down into their reserves and the Czechs did not get a single shot on goal while Mara was off.

With five minutes left to play, Flyer Frank Dunster took a minor penalty. Goaltender Murray Dowey was forced to turn aside four rapid-fire shots.

Canadian Press reported: "on territorial play, the Canadians looked at least a goal better than the Czechs and on today's showing they reigned favourites to win the tournament".

An Ottawa newspaper crowed:

CRACK CZECH SQUAD HELD TO SCORELESS TIE

Czechoslovakia's high scoring forward, Vladimir Zabrodsky, who finished the tournament as top scorer with 27 goals, was kept off the score sheet.

Zabrodsky didn't play well in games when there was physical contact and heavy body checking.

In the game with the United States, he took a huge hit from an American defenceman. For the rest of the game he didn't stray within five strides of the puck and didn't even earn an assist.

Frank Boucher cautiously said: "I think we have a good chance of taking it".

A crowd of 2,500 watched the game in Olympic Stadium.

Czech coach Mike Buchna, from Trail, B.C., said after the game: "It's real playoff hockey".

SUMMARY – GAME SIX
RCAF FLYERS vs. CZECHOSLOVAKIA

First Period
Scoring: None
Penalty – Mara

Second Period
Scoring: None
Penalties – Laperriere, Rozinak

Third Period
Scoring: None
Penalties – Mara, Sluma, Dunster

# GAME SEVEN
## RCAF FLYERS vs. AUSTRIA
RCAF FLYERS   12   AUSTRIA  0

Austria was next to fall before the high scoring Flyers.

Murray Dowey racked up his fourth shutout in seven games as Flyers shellacked Austria 12-0 in a swirling snowstorm.

Wally Halder led the attack with four goals and three assists. George Mara also had four goals and Reg Schroeter fired a hat trick. Ab Renaud scored the 12th goal.

The game was penalty free.

That morning Czechoslovakia defeated Switzerland 7-1.

Flyers' win set the stage for a crucial game against Switzerland the next day. The Czechs had a relatively soft game with the United States remaining. Flyers were tied with the Czechs, both with six wins and a tie.

A loss by Canada would mean the Gold Medal would go to the Czechs. A Czech loss to the United States and a Flyers' win against Switzerland would mean Gold for Canada.

If Canada and Czechoslovakia remained tied at the top of the heap, the Gold Medal would go to the team with the best Goals For and Against quotient.

Canada had a 66-5 record for a quotient of 13.2. The Czechs scored more goals – 76 – but allowed 15 and their quotient was only 5.06. Flyers had to win and they had to bar the door. There was an outside chance they could win against Switzerland but still lose the Gold Medal if they allowed too many goals in their last game.

## SUMMARY – GAME SEVEN

First Period

1.                    Canada         –          Halder
1:00
2.  Canada – Schroeter (Halder)                     4:10
3.                    Canada         –          Halder
9:38
4.          Canada       -          Mara      (Guzzo)
14:48
5.                    Canada         –          Schroeter
 16:30
Penalties – None

Second Period

6.                    Canada         –          Halder
:50
7.          Canada       –       Schroeter    (Halder)
1:40
8.                    Canada         -          Mara
 3:10
9.          Canada       -          Renaud     (Halder)

6:13

10. Canada – Mara
15:10

Penalties – None

Third Period

11. Canada – Mara (Guzzo)
:40

12. Canada - Halder
4:08

Penalties – None

# GAME EIGHT
## RCAF FLYERS vs. SWITZERLAND
## RCAF FLYERS 3   SWITZERLAND 0

The quest for Olympic Gold came down to the last two games – Canada vs Switzerland and the Czechs vs the U.S.

The Flyers defeated Switzerland and did it in Gold Medal fashion – a 3-0 shutout. The outcome of the Czech-U.S. game was now of no consequence. There was no way the Czechs could possibly match the Flyers final quotient of 13.8. The Czechs managed to eke out a slim 4-3 victory over the American squad.

Canada and Czechoslovakia finished the tournament undefeated – both with seven wins and a tie – but the Czechs had to be satisfied with Silver.

Wally Halder scored the winning goal – his 21st of the Olympics – at 4:23 of the first period. Patsy Guzzo, with an assist from George Mara, scored the insurance goal at 3:13 of the second period. He took a pass from Mara, slipped around his opposing wingman, split the defence, deked the goaltender to his knees and picked a corner. It would have been a pretty goal under perfect ice conditions. Patsy's moves were spectacular considering a hot sun was beating down and turning the ice surface into heavy slush.

Reg Schroeter put the game out of reach at 7:34 of the third period.

Reg Schroeter's shot "skipped like a stone over water and then skipped over the goalie's stick," Canadian Press writer Jack Sullivan wrote.

Canadian Press reported the rink was a sea of slush and that Canada had to overcome partisan refereeing. Play had to be stopped every ten minutes so players could clean off the ice. "Sandy" Watson remembers, "the weather was mild and a game had been played on the rink just before ours. I couldn't believe my eyes. There was at least two inches of slush on the surface. There was so much slush on the ice that Ted Hibberd would tee up the puck like a golf ball and golf it down the ice. Our boys didn't skate down the ice. They ran down it."

The hometown Swiss crowd showered the Flyers with snowballs and bottles.

There was a non-starter suggestion that the game be suspended and resumed the next day but that was not in the cards. The next day, Hubie Brooks was being married and the entire team was invited. Olympic organizers vetoed the suggestion the game be played the following day in Zurich because thousands had already made travel plans to return home.

CP writer Jack Sullivan, probably the only western reporter at the Olympics, wrote: "the ice conditions were so bad that at times the game threatened to develop into a farce. The officials, Eric de Marcwicz of Britain and Van Reyshoot of Belgium were pointedly in favour of Switzerland, some of the latter's decisions being almost unbelievable."

Wally Halder attempted to check a Swiss player, missed and fell flat. The Swiss player also went down – he either fell down or took a dive. Halder was given a major penalty by Van Reyshoot – "for tripping and interference".

Halder told reporters later "if you tried to get even, you'd set up a guy for a body-check and off you'd go. Body-checking as the Olympic referees rule, is taboo. Then, too, the further we went without a loss, the worse it got".

Ted Hibberd was crosschecked from behind and fell heavily to the ice. Both players were thumbed off with minor penalties.

Murray Dowey recalls that "near the end of the game there was a scramble in front of my net and Swiss player, Heinrich Boller, punched me in the face when I was down. He was only given a two-minute penalty. I decided to keep my mouth shut or I'd probably end up in the penalty box with him for talking".

Trainer George McFaul said after the game: "we played eight men, the Swiss players and the referees."

During the second and third periods the partisan Swiss crowd voiced their displeasure at some of the referees' calls.

Jack Sullivan wrote that Wally Halder's winning goal "was the neatest of the tournament.

"He literally ran over the slushy ice, traveling the length of the rink to fire a low corner shot that the Swiss goaltender managed to kick out. Three Swiss players jostled him, but he grabbed the rebound and fired again. The netminder deflected the puck behind the net and Schroeter returned it to Halder who, though, still hemmed in by three rivals, banged it in."

Murray Dowey finished strongly with five shutouts. It might have been six if he hadn't had that momentary lapse in the 21-1 win against Italy.

His scoreless streak over the last four games extended over 195 minutes and :30 seconds.

His last three games were shutouts.

The last goal scored on him was by the United States at 4:30 of the third period in Game Five.

The team that had been written off was now being lionized.

They had been undefeated in eight games. They had won Gold.

Marcel Heninger, Chairman of the Swiss Olympic Committee, presented each player with a Gold Medal in a burgundy leather case.

Murray Dowey stood next to George Mara during the medal presentation. George turned to Murray and said: "This is the proudest moment of my life".

"Sandy" Watson declared the Flyers to be "the best team in the world".

Coach Frank Boucher told the players: "Fellows, I am proud of you. I want to thank you all and that goes for the boys who didn't play. You're a great gang and I knew you'd do it."

The Flyers received congratulatory telegrams from around the world, including one from Prime Minister Wlliam Lyon Mackenzie King.

What had to be the classiest telegram was one from the British team, Olympic champions in 1936 and defending World and Olympic title holders: "CONGRATULATIONS TO THE NEW CHAMPIONS FROM   THE EX-

152

Young External Affairs diplomat, Lester B. (Mike) Pearson, said:
"What you did was the greatest diplomatic feat of any group from Canada in my experience"

Back home, the next day the Ottawa Journal's Page One headline read:
 FLYERS BRING TITLE BACK
TO CRADLE OF GAME
RAGS TO RICHES SAGA
CLIMAXED BY VICTORY

The Flyers were wandering around in a daze. All 33-year old Louis Lecompte could say was: "I never thought an old man would be an Olympic champion".

For a change, "Red" Gravelle was absolutely speechless. All he could muster was: "Am I proud! Am I proud! Am I proud."

Canada's House of Commons had just voted O Canada to be the nation's National Anthem but nobody bothered to tell the IOC or the Swiss. When the Flyers lined up to receive their Gold Medals, the band struck up with The Maple Leaf Forever.

"Sandy" Watson shepherded the players back on the ice for a victory photo. Just before the photographer clicked his shutter, team members yelled: "Hold it, hold it". They wanted CAHA Registrar George Dudley in the photo. And so, a proud George Dudley stood next to "Sandy" and his jubilant Flyers.

George McFaul took down the Canadian flag and draped it on the team bus. En route to their hotel, someone tried to steal the flag from the bus. "Red" Gravelle attempted to grab the would-be-thief but the bus was already moving again.

After a shower, RCAF Group Captain Robert Thompson threw a party for the team.

The Canadian ski team was invited.

The Wurtele twins, Rhona and Rhoda, from Montreal were there. So were Gaby Bleau from Montreal and Harvey Clifford from Ottawa.

Then, George Dudley and team players traded war stories and took shots at their ordeal by fire.

Earlier on, Patsy Guzzo had written a letter to Ottawa Journal sports editor, Tommy Shields. Shields printed the letter under the head:

REFEREEING IN EUROPE
DEPLORED BY PATSY GUZZO

"We are forced to play in rain or snow under European rules which are most confusing and in games refereed by the most incompetent arbiters you ever hope to see.

"The refereeing here in Europe has been one continuous nightmare. We have been kicked and slashed all over the ice and holding and interference are condoned by all referees so far."

Patsy Guzzo's letter dated January 30, 1948

George Dudley went further and he spoke with the weight and authority of the Canadian Amateur Hockey Association behind him.

He spoke of "ridiculous weather conditions" and "inexperienced and incompetent referees."

He heaped withering scorn on "watery ice, deep slush and games played in snowstorms" and pledged that "never again" would a team from Canada compete unless games were played on artificial ice in covered arenas.

SUMMARY – GAME EIGHT
RCAF FLYERS vs. SWITZERLAND

First Period
1. Canada – Halder (Schroeter) 4:23
Penalties – Lecompte, Halder (major)

Second Period
2. Canada – Guzzo (Mara) 3:13
Penalties – Boller (2), Laperriere, Trepp, U. Poltero,
Durst, Halder, Gravelle

Third Period
3. Canada – Schroeter
7:34
Penalties – Boller, Ruedi, Hibberd, Laperriere,
Gravelle, Halder

FINAL STANDINGS

| | W | L | T | GF | GA |
|---|---|---|---|---|---|
| Canada | 7 | 0 | 1 | 69 | 5 |
| Czechoslovakia | 7 | 0 | 1 | 80 | 18 |
| Switzerland | 6 | 2 | 0 | 67 | 21 |
| *USA | 5 | 3 | 0 | 86 | 33 |
| Sweden | 4 | 4 | 0 | 55 | 28 |
| Great Britain | 3 | 5 | 0 | 39 | 47 |
| Poland | 2 | 6 | 0 | 20 | 97 |
| Austria | 1 | 7 | 0 | 33 | 77 |
| Italy | 0 | 8 | 0 | 24 | 156 |

THE SCORES
| | | |
|---|---|---|
| January 30 | Canada 3 | Sweden 1 |
| February 1 | Canada 3 | England 0 |
| February 2 | Canada 15 | Poland 0 |
| February 3 | Canada 21 | Italy 1 |

February 5            Canada 12    USA 3*
February 6            Canada 0     Czechoslovakia 0
February 7            Canada 12    Austria 0
February 8            Canada 3     Switzerland 0
GOALS                 FOR  69      AGAINST 5**

\* Worst beating ever administered to a US team.
\*\* Five shutouts – an Olympic record.

Wally Halder, George Mara, Reg Schroeter and Ab Renaud were 1-2-3-4 in Flyers' goal production. They accounted for 54 of the team's 69 goals. Ab Renaud's 10 assists still stand as an Olympic hockey record.

## THE SCORERS

| | GAMES | GOALS | ASSISTS | POINTS |
|---|---|---|---|---|
| Wally Halder | 8 | 21 | 8 | 29 |
| George Mara | 8 | 8 | 17 | 9   26 |
| Reg Schroeter | 8 | 12 | 5 | 17 |
| Ab Renaud | 8 | 4 | 10 | 14 |
| Patsy Guzzo | 8 | 5 | 7 | 12 |
| Ted Hibberd | 8 | 3 | 4 | 7 |
| Louis Lecompte | 8 | 2 | 3 | 5 |
| "Red" Gravelle | 7 | 3 | 0 | 3 |
| Andre Laperriere | 8 | 1 | 1 | 2 |

| | | | |
|---|---|---|---|
| Frank Dunster | 8 | 1 | 0 |
| 1 | | | |
| Irving Taylor | 1 | 0 | 0 |
| 0 | | | |
| Murray Dowey | 8 | 0 | 0 |
| 0 | | | |


MacKENZIE KING TELEGRAM

Squadron Leader A.G. Watson

Manager,

Canadian Olympic Hockey Team

St. Moritz

WORD HAS JUST BEEN RECEIVED THAT CANADIAN

OLYMPIC HOCKEY TEAM HAS WON THE OLYMPIC

HOCKEY TITLE THE VICTORY OF OUR TEAM WILL BE

RECEIVED WITH REJOICING THROUGHOUT ALL

PARTS OF CANADA ON BEHALF OF THE GOVERNMENT

AND THE PEOPLE OF CANADA I SEND TO YOURSELF

AND MEMBERS OF THE TEAM HEARTIEST CONGRATULATIONS ON THE TEAMS SPLENDID

ACHIEVEMENT IN WINNING THE OLYMPIC CHAMPIONSHIP


W L MACKENZIE KING

# THE FLYERS:

## AB RENAUD

Ab Renaud was every coach's dream player – up and down his wing, checking his opposite number and displaying consistent scoring punch. He was only 165-pounds but he didn't back away from a physical game. He was solid. He was sturdy. He was steady. He didn't give the puck away. He didn't make mistakes.

He was a "Westboro boy," born in Ottawa's west end in 1920. He played his junior and senior hockey in the Ottawa area.

During World War Two he served overseas as a Sergeant with the Medical Corps. When he was honourably discharged he began a career in the federal public service with Veterans' Affairs but shortly afterwards transferred to the Department of Agriculture.

He didn't take in the Flyers losses to McGill and Ottawa Army at the Auditorium but "I knew a couple of the guys who were trying out with the team."

He was playing on the first line with Reg Schroeter and Ted Hibberd with Burghs in the strong Ottawa Senior League. Their line was among the league leading scorers.

"We were leading the league. In our first nine games we won six, lost two and tied one".

"One day I got a call from Bill Gould, the executive assistant to the Deputy Minister, Dr. Barton. He asked me to come to his office. He told me they had received a call from Defence Minister Brooke Claxton's executive assistant and the RCAF Flyers were interested in me joining the team.

"They also wanted Frank Dunster, Ted Hibberd, Pete Leichnitz and Reg Schroeter. I was definitely interested.

"'Sandy' Watson called me and I went over to his office in temporary building "B" on Cartier Square. I had been a Sergeant in the Army during the war and the best "Sandy" could offer me was Corporal in the RCAF.

"I'd end up taking a pay cut if I accepted. Then, "Sandy" threw in trades' pay, which brought me up to Sergeant's pay.

I was single. Money wasn't really that important. I'd have played for nothing."

Ab was injured in the Flyers' exhibition game against the Ottawa Senior League's RCAF team.

The ocean crossing on the Queen Elizabeth gave him precious time to nurse his injured knee.

He tested his knee at a practice in Streatham shortly after arriving in London and pronounced himself fit.

His medical problems didn't end there.

Shortly after eating a hotel meal, he complained of a stomach ache.

"Sandy" Watson deemed the ailment serious enough to have him taken to a London area military hospital.

Ab overheard "Sandy" asking where surgical operations were performed. He thought perhaps he was suffering from appendicitis.

"Anyway, my tummy ache disappeared and my knee was fit so I didn't miss a game".

His hockey career in Ottawa began in 1936 with Woodroffe Juveniles. He played with Lasalle Juniors in 1937-39 and with Hull Volants Senior "A" team in 1940-41.

He played with a Canadian Army team in England in 1945, with Ottawa Senators in 1946 and Ottawa Montagnards in 1947.

After the Olympics, he played with Ottawa RCAF in the Eastern League in 1949-50 and with Army in 1951.

He was player-coach with Brockville in the New York-Ontario league between 1952 and 1957.

When Barbara Ann Scott won her Gold Medal in St. Moritz, Ab and Reg Schroeter were standing by the rink boards.

"The runner-up, a U.S. skater, fell on her fanny three times and got soaked.

"The photographers all crowded around Barbara Ann for photos and her mother said to us 'pick her up and put her on your shoulders'. We did and the picture was flashed around the world.

"Reg had a chocolate bar and he passed it up to her. Barbara Ann said 'this must be hard on you' and Reg answered: 'Don't worry. We like it'."

In May, 2004, Ottawa's Minto Skating Club celebrated its 100th Birthday and Barbara Ann Scott and Tommy King flew in from Florida for the occasion.

Barb asked me if I could arrange a reunion with surviving Flyers and their families. I contacted Ab and he volunteered his golf club, Rivermead, as a venue.

Barb and Tommy and my wife, Janet, and I drove over to the club on the Aylmer Road on the Quebec side of the Ottawa River.

The Flyers' "family" was assembled and waiting.

Ab and his new bride, Lorraine, were there. So was Reg Schroeter's widow, Shirley; "Sandy" Watson's widow, Pat; Ted Hibberd, Frank Boucher's daughter, Diane, and Ottawa Sun columnist Earl McRae.

Earl suggested that Ab and Ted recreate the famous photo of Ab and Reg Schroeter hoisting Barbara Ann up on their shoulders and they obliged. Actually, they fudged the shot. Barb stood between them so that it appeared she was resting on their shoulders.

When you are in your early 80s you avoid lifting – even though Barbara Ann only weighed 96 pounds, the same as she weighed when she won Canada's only ladies' Gold figure skating medal.

Ab has been a longtime member of the Rivermead Golf Club and can be found there most fine summer days.

He married, for the first time, when he was 80. His bride, Lorraine, was a widow and a longtime friend.

Shortly after his marriage, Ab participated in the annual Oldtimers' Hockey Golf Tournament at Ottawa's Highlands' Golf Club.

The irreverent tournament program related that Ab and Lorraine were living in Ab's old family home on Princeton Street in Ottawa's west end because "they wanted to be close to the schools."

Ab also belongs to a select club of 15 former athletes and retired businessmen.

The members "chip in" $30 a month each and rent a large room on the second floor of a low-rise commercial building on Richmond Road in the west end.

The club is called "Smuckers."

Larry Reagan, Calder Trophy winner and Jack Kent Cooke's General Manager of the Los Angeles Kings, belongs. So does Sam Gaw, a former semi-pro player whose son played for the Ottawa 67s' Junior squad.

They meet every afternoon for a few hours of friendly Gin Rummy.

When they formed the club, their old friend, Harry Koffman, Ottawa leading sign painter, volunteered he would design their artwork and logo and that he would donate a sign.

Sitting down for breakfast one morning, Harry's wife placed a jar of Smucker's marmalade on the table. That was Harry's inspiration.

"I will call them Smuckers because they are all schmucks."

Member Gerry Dover is the retired owner of a small family owned hardware store. Ray Sally is the retired owner/manager of one of Ottawa's largest independent travel agencies.

Lude Check played for New York Rovers, Sydney Millionaires, North Sydney Victorias and for eight seasons in the Quebec Senior League with Quebec Aces and Ottawa Senators.

In 1943-44, Detroit Red Wings brought him up from Quebec Aces for one game.

In 1944-45 he played 26 games with Chicago Black Hawks and scored six goals.

"Chick" Wolfe is the retired owner of one of Ottawa's best-known shoe stores.

Smuckers' rules are few but simple – no alcoholic beverages on the premises or no gambling for money.

The members feel if these two basic rules are followed, they need have no fear of being raided by the local constabulary.

The fridge is stocked with soft drinks and bottled war and there is an overhead TV set for viewing major sporting events. Otherwise, the room is decorated in what one of the members calls "early Salvation Army."

There is hardly a square inch on the walls that is not covered by photos and news stories of members.

Ab Renaud was Flyers' fourth highest point getter in the Olympics. He scored four goals and led all Olympic scorers with a high of 10 assists.

When the team returned home to Ottawa they were given, according to "Sandy" Watson, "a splendid lunch" at Beaver Barracks. Ab Renaud recalls: "I had a beer with Justice Minister Louis St. Laurent who was representing the Prime Minister."

## ANDRE LAPERRIERE

Flyers' defenceman, Andre Laperriere, is in the Olympics' record books with a record that will never be matched.

He has the lowest goals against average – 0.00 – of any Olympic netminder. He also holds the record for the least time spent in the nets – eight seconds.

In the game against Sweden, Murray Dowey was penalized for gloving a shot and throwing the puck forward. The rules stipulated he could only throw the puck to the side of the net or behind it. Murray had to leave the ice, go to the penalty box and serve a two-minute minor penalty.

Canada was leading 3-1 and there were eight seconds remaining in the game.

Coach Frank Boucher called a huddle at the bench and asked if anyone wanted to volunteer to go in the nets.

No one did until Andre Laperriere said: "What the heck. I'm a defenceman and I've blocked a few shots. I'll do it.

163

"So, I took Murray's trapper and blocker and his stick and finished the game. The Swedes didn't get a shot on me."

The penalty box was next door to the Flyers' bench. As Murray took his seat on the bench, a sarcastic Coach Boucher said: "Nice throw, Murray, but why'd ya do it?" Murray broke down and began sobbing.

Andre was the Flyers' most penalized player. He was assessed seven minor penalties but he was not a dirty player. His teammates say that most of the penalties called by European referees would not have been called in a typical senior game in Canada.

Andre was a 22-year old, 170-pound defenceman at the University of Montreal. He played Varsity hockey for five years in an intercollegiate loop that included McGill, Laval, Queen's and University of Toronto.

"We won the intercollegiate championship in two of the years I played. I knew Wally Halder from college hockey. I played against him when he played for Toronto Varsity."

While attending University of Montreal, Andre was a reservist with Le Regiment de Maisonneuve and trained with them at Farnham, Quebec.

Andre was at home one Sunday in December, 1947, "having supper with my family. The phone rang and it was for me". My mother said: "c'est un Anglais pour vous."

"It was Mr. Dawe, Vice President of the Canadian Amateur Hockey Association.

"He asked me I wanted to play for Canada in the Olympics in Switzerland. I told him I'd talk it over with my family and get back to him. He said he had to know then and there and that he would call me back in 15 minutes.

"My father advised me it was a great honor, a once in a lifetime opportunity and I should not pass it up.

"So, when Mr. Dawe called back 15 minutes later I told him I was in. He told me to be at Dorval airport at 7.00 the next morning.

"When I got out to Dorval, an airman approached me and asked: 'Laperriere?' Then he led me aboard a twin engine RCAF plane. I was the only passenger.

"I still feel badly over when I arrived in Ottawa. The airman who met me was the defenceman who was cut to make room for me."

## ANDY GILPIN

Andy Gilpin was in Whitehorse when "I received an invitation to attend a western Canada tryout camp for the 1948 RCAF Olympic hockey team.

"Except for the odd recreational game on a pond I had been out of hockey for a year but I went to Edmonton anyway.

"Only three of us – Len Beatch, Ross King and your truly – made the cut and were flown to Ottawa to parade our skills before Frank Boucher."

Andy Gilpin was born in Montreal and played Junior "A" there.

He tried out with the Senior Montreal Royals and was one of their last cuts.

"I worked at Crain's plumbing factory with Maurice "Rocket" Richard and Pat Desbiens. When Crain's moved into making munitions, I enlisted in the RCAF in 1940. I was a technician and I served at

Pat Bay, B.C., and in the Aleutians. I was 'demobbed' in 1945 and moved to Abbotsford, B.C. My job at Crain's was waiting for me but I left to work for War Assets Disposal.

"I re-enlisted in the RCAF in 1947 and was posted to Whitehorse."

He played senior and services' hockey.

"I remember once I scored a hat trick against "Chuck" Rayner when he was playing for the Navy team. I put a different 'deke' on him each time. He was some sore. Our team in Pat Bay had six NHL players on it."

Andy Gilpin was one of Frank Boucher's "Black Aces" – one of five players who did not dress for any of the Flyers' eight Olympic contests.

The Flyers carried 17 men on their roster but only 11 could dress for a game. Irving Taylor was inserted in the line-up for the opening game only. He was benched in favour of Orval "Red" Gravelle who played the seven remaining games.

Goaltender Ross King, forwards Hubie Brooks, Andy Gilpin and Pete Leichnitz and defenceman Roy Forbes watched the Olympic hockey games as spectators. They did see ice-time in the 34 exhibition games the Flyers played in England and Europe.

Frank Boucher says it was "a tough decision to bench five good players – probably the toughest decision I was ever called on to make."

Andy Gilpin remembers one exhibition game in Sweden.

"My upper lip was cut by a high stick and I took two stitches. Trainer George McFaul laid out one of Dr. Watson's sterile suture kits and he sewed me up right there at the bench. I went back out the next shift and got the winning goal.

166

"I guess that today an NHL player who gets clipped by a high stick would be taken to the rink clinic, maybe to a hospital. He might miss the next day's practice or maybe even the next game."

Frank Boucher refers to today's NHL players as "highly paid and highly pampered".

After the Olympics, Andy stayed in the RCAF and continued to play hockey with RCAF teams.

"I played on a line with "Red" Gravelle and Tony Licari.

He retired from the RCAF in 1975 and settled in the Trenton-Belleville area. He now lives near London, Ontario.


## FRANK DUNSTER
### DISTINGUISHED FLYING CROSS

Frank Dunster was the only player to have been awarded the Distinguished Flying Cross during World War Two.

He was born in the village of Richmond, just outside Ottawa, in 1921.

His dream of a career as a professional hockey player was cut short by war.

The Oshawa Generals were the first junior team to win back-to-back Memorial Cups in 1939 and 1940.

In 1939, Billy (The Kid) Taylor was a one-man wrecking crew as Oshawa swept Edmonton in four straight games.

Taylor scored nine goals and assisted on six others.

Frank Dunster was a defenceman on the 1940 club. Billy Taylor was gone but the Generals clawed past Toronto Young Rangers, Toronto Marlboros,

South Porcupine Dome Miners and Verdun Maple Leafs to reach the Memorial Cup for the third straight year.

Their opponent was the Kenora Thistles club led by goaltender Chuck Rayner and defenceman Bill Juzda.

Kenora managed to win only one game.

Frank Dunster enlisted in the RCAF March 30, 1942. He was commissioned as a Pilot Officer in April, 1944.

He flew 200 operational hours as bomb aimer-navigator on Halifax bombers.

The Halifax was the workhorse of the RCAF. It was used on U-Boat patrols, for dropping paratroops, for laying mines in fjords, as an air ambulance, for glider towing and as a heavy night bomber.

A Halifax bomber carried a crew of six to eight, had a maximum speed of 280 mph, a ceiling of 22,800 feet and a range of 3,000 miles. It was very lightly armored with ten .303 caliber machine guns – four tail guns, two nose guns and four dorsal guns.

A Halifax bomber carried six and a half tons of bombs.

Halifax bombers flew 75,532 sorties during World War Two.

Only four made it to 100 missions. Aside from the fact it presented a lumbering target, the Halifax had a design flaw. If it was flung about in the sky to avoid searchlights or ack ack batteries it sometimes went into an uncontrollable spin.

Frank Dunster flew 37 bombing missions over Berlin, Essen and Cologne in Halifax bombers – one complete tour of duty plus seven. He was awarded the Distinguished Flying Cross on March 15, 1945.

There is not one air-worthy Halifax bomber remaining anywhere in the world. A museum in Yorkshire has a shell with many non-Halifax components. The Royal Air Force Museum in Hendon has one fished out of a Norwegian fjord. It is on display in its crashed condition. The RCAF Museum in Trenton has a partially restored one.

After his honorable discharge Frank settled down to civilian life back in Ottawa. He joined the Ottawa Fire Department as a firefighter. He played amateur hockey in the four team Ottawa Senior League – Ottawa Army coached by Bill Cowley, Ottawa RCAF managed by "Sandy" Watson, Hull and New Edinburgh "Burghs".

When it became apparent that the RCAF Flyers needed more firepower, Frank was one of five Burghs' players invited to join the club. The four others were Reg Schroeter, Ab Renaud, Pete Leichnitz and Ted Hibberd.

Dunster went to Ottawa Fire Chief Gray Burnett to ask for leave to join the team. His request was denied. So, Dunster quit the Fire Department and re-enlisted in the RCAF. He was given his old rank back.

Ab Renaud recalls that Frank Dunster was "a defenceman who liked to hit. He was a tremendous hip-checker." Body checking was not de rigeur in European hockey and Dunster was whistled off four times for clean body checks.

When the Olympic Games and exhibition tour ended, he remained in the RCAF. He flew in everything the RCAF had – including CF 100s as a navigator – until his retirement as a Flight Lieutenant.

Frank Dunster died from cancer April 8, 1995, at age 74.

## GEORGE MARA

George Mara was a natural. Murray Dowey rates him as one of the greatest puck handlers and stick handlers he ever saw. He said that George could hang on to a puck forever – if he chose to.

George toyed with hockey. It was not the most important compartment in his multi-faceted life. He did it his way and on his terms.

Mara was playing Junior "B" in the Ontario Hockey Association with Upper Canada College when he was 15. His coach was Joe Primeau. He scored 16 goals in six league games and four more in three playoff games.

He had two five-goal games and one four-goal game against University of Toronto Schools and a four-goal game against Aurora in a playoff game in Maple Leaf Gardens.

Detroit Red Wings placed the up and coming prospect on their negotiating list.

In 1941 he played with the Junior "A' Marlboros on a team with Bob Goldham and Gaye Stewart.

When war broke out, he enlisted in the Royal Canadian Navy. While he was at Signal School in St. Hyacinthe, Frank Selke contacted him and invited him to play with Montreal Royals.

After the war ended and players returned home, NHL negotiating lists were scrapped and George became a free agent.

He tried out for the Maple Leafs, along with 57 others, but was cut by Conn Smythe and "Hap" Day.

Detroit Red Wings grabbed him up. Jim Norris, Sr. and Jack Adams wanted him to suit up for the Stanley Cup playoffs against Toronto but George talked it over with his father and decided he did not want to play "any place but Toronto." Detroit was up 3-0 in games against the Leafs and Toronto came back to win the next four games and the Stanley Cup.

In 1946, along with Wally Halder, he attended New York Rangers' tryout camp in Winnipeg. Rangers offered him a $7,500 no-trade, no-cut contract – an unheard of sum for a rookie – and he turned it down.

"I didn't want to play hockey in New York."

Meanwhile, he was being groomed to take over the family wine importing business.

In 1892, an article in the now extinct newspaper, The World, described "The Wm. Mara Company" as having "the largest wine vaults in Canada." The vaults occupied an entire city block in the King and Yonge Streets area.

Newspaper ads in The Mail list seven-year old Canadian whiskey for $3.00 a gallon and premium Rye for $3.75 a gallon. Mara's Special Blend was sold in one-gallon stone crocks.

George's connections with the wine and spirits industry in Europe would later serve the Flyers well.

"I remember one day in 1947 I was at Maple Leaf Gardens picking up my hockey tickets and I ran into W.E. Hewitt, Foster's father. I asked him how he was and he said, "we are in a mess." He was referring to the RCAF Flyers' team after they lost their first two exhibition games big-time. He said they were trying to find reinforcements.

"So, I suggested Wally Halder and Murray Dowey. His eyes lit up and he took off like a scalded cat. A couple of days later, Wally called me and said he received an invitation from the Flyers but he didn't think he could get the time off work. He was working in sales and marketing for the E.P. Taylor conglomerate – Barker's Biscuits, Willard's Chocolates, Suchard Chocolate.

"I promised him I'd phone Eddy Taylor. I did and Wally got the time off. Then, I said to myself 'what the hell, Wally's going. Why am I not going, too?"

Ab Renaud remembers the day George Mara and Wally Halder showed up at the Auditorium to join the team: "They were both driving 1948 Buick convertibles. That's the same car the City of Ottawa tried to give Barbara Ann Scott but she had to give it back or she'd lose her amateur status."

George was the Flyers' second highest scorer – three points behind Wally Halder. He had 17 goals and nine assists. In one game he scored twice within a 13 second span. In the game against Italy, Mara, Halder and Schroeter scored three goals in 59 seconds.

The 1948 Olympics produced many urban legends. One of them is about Halder and Mara. When the Games ended, "Sandy" Watson reached into his poke and gave each player $200 to buy souvenirs in Switzerland.

The pair left the team early to return to Toronto for Barker's Biscuits' mercantile hockey league playoffs.

En route, they stopped in on a racetrack in Paris, pooled their $200 gratuities and bet $400 on a long shot.

The horse came in first and paid a king's ransom. Halder and Mara donated their winnings to the Canadian Olympic committee and the Olympic Trust was born.

George Mara laughs when the legend is repeated to him. Then, he launches into his association with the Trust.

"In 1970, Canada's Olympic committee was broke. I think they owed a quarter of a million dollars. They came to me and asked me if I could bail them out. I wanted to help but I really didn't have the time the job would demand.

"So, I drew up a job description that I thought would be impossible for them to accept. It was "I", "I", "I". "I" would be all-powerful. I submitted it to them. I was in France, staying in a Hennessy chateau in Cognac, when the Toronto Star called me: 'Mr. Mara, how does it feel to be the new Czar of amateur sport in Canada?'

"They bought my proposal and job description 100 percent.

"A couple of weeks later, I was playing tennis with Wally Halder and I asked him how things were at Vickers and Benson, the advertising agency where he was working. He said he wasn't too happy and I asked him: "How'd you like to be President of the Olympic Trust?'

"He held that position for the next 24 years".

After the 1948 Games, Frank Selke contacted him and offered him $10,000 to finish out the season with the Montreal Royals and play with Montreal Canadiens in the Stanley Cup playoffs.

George commuted from Toronto and played the last seven games of the schedule with the Royals. He scored three goals and picked up five assists. Dickie Moore, "Boom Boom" Geoffrion, Camille Henri, Tom Manastersky, Gordie Knutson and Bert Hirschfield all played two or three games with the Royals but none managed to score.

George Mara remembers his very last game of pro hockey:

"It was the very last game of the season. Cliff Malone, our leading scorer, had 34 goals and 60 assists, and he was trying to lock up the league scoring title.

"There were five or six seconds to go and I put a sure goal on Cliff's stick. An opposing player hit me and almost put me through the end of the rink. I went down.

"I was out cold. My shoulder was separated. I was in terrible pain.

"The first thing I heard and saw when I recovered consciousness was Cliff standing over me saying: 'Don't worry, I scored!'

"I was in such excruciating agony I couldn't have cared less.

"I was strapped up for about 10 weeks and never did get to play with the Canadiens. Then and there, I decided to hang up the blades."

George continued to climb the corporate ladder in Toronto and served, at one time, as Chairman of Maple Leaf Gardens.

He is the only Flyer in the Olympic Hall of Fame. He was named in the Builder category because of his association with the Olympic Trust.

When asked where his Olympic Gold Medal was – at home? in a safety deposit box?, he guffawed: "Gold, my medal is made of lead. I had it inserted in a puck and it is in my den at home."

When questioned: "Are you sure it is not gold?" he replied: "I know gold when I see it." When his story was repeated to Ab Renaud and "Sandy" Watson they said: "George is pulling your leg! Call him back."

No, he wasn't pulling my leg. He was adamant that his medal was lead coloured to look like gold. Could it be that when he was presented with his medal in the small leather box he was given a Silver Medal by mistake?

George Mara passed away in Toronto on August 30, 2006, 3½ months short of his 85th birthday.

## ROY FORBES

Roy Forbes was born April 6, 1922, in Rorketon, Manitoba, a small community north east of Dauphin.

His military career spanned 40 years beginning with service with the Manitoba Mounted Rifles non-permanent active militia in 1940.

He was honorably released and joined the Royal Canadian Air Force in April, 1942. He graduated as an air bomber in August, 1943, and was posted overseas in October.

He flew operations on Lancaster bombers over northwest Europe as a member of 419 (Moose) Squadron.

His seventh mission in a Lancaster was as a bomb aimer near Cambrai, France. His squadron was bombing ahead of advancing Allied troops shortly after D-Day.

"There was cloud cover so we were flying below the cloud level at 1,200 to 1,300 feet. We were hit. I think it was a night fighter than got us. We got the order to jump. I jumped at about 800 feet – not even high enough for my 'chute to open fully.

"I landed on my feet. I was on the loose– alone – for two weeks – rain, no food – always on edge. I ate grass, roots and bark. I spent two weeks walking towards Caen.

"After two weeks some Catholic nuns befriended me and turned me over to the local Resistance. I was with the Underground for four months. I was passed along the French-Belgian escape underground. In one village – Auchy les Mines in France – they had me living in a room above a pub. There were Germans in the village.

"After four months with the Underground I was linked up with a Scots' Highland armored unit. I was returned to England and in October, 1944, I was back in Canada. The RCAF posted me back to England and operational duties in March, 1945.

"In October, 1945, I was given my honorable discharge and released from the RCAF. I transferred to the RCAF reserve but in 1947 I transferred back in the RCAF regular force."

Roy Forbes played for Portage la Prairie Terriers when they defeated Oshawa Generals for the Memorial Cup in 1942. The Terriers entered the Memorial Cup final riding a 22-game winning streak.

Staff Sergeant Addie Bell coached the Terriers and two of his sons, goaltender Gordon Bell and forward Joe Bell, played on the team. Portage la Prairie won the first two games 5-1 and 8-7 but their win streak was stopped at 24 when Oshawa won Game Three. An 8-2 rout in Game Four earned Portage the Memorial Cup.

During one of his postings in the Maritimes, Roy played senior hockey with the Truro Bearcats.

As a Leading Aircraftsman, when Roy Forbes boarded the Queen Elizabeth in New York, he quipped: "this is a bit different than the last time I crossed on the Lizzie. I was lugging a kit bag then."

After the St. Moritz Games, he was transferred to Rockcliffe air station, Ottawa, as a meteorological observer from 1948 to 1951.

"Along with most of the Ottawa crowd I played with the RCAF in the Eastern Canada Hockey League made up of North Bay, Cornwall, Pembroke, Hull, RCAF and Army. I played with the RCAF from 1948 to 1950 and with Army, '50-51."

According to Roy, the Army was still sensitive over the fact that the 1948 Olympic team was not a Tri-Services team and there was no Army presence. Ab Renaud and Murray Dowey served in the Army during World War Two but had to re-enlist with the RCAF and wear air force blue. Wally Halder and George Mara served as naval officers during the war but elected to play with the 1948 RCAF Flyers as civilians. Roy says the Army was determined it was going to ice a team to represent Canada at the 1952 Olympics in Oslo.

"I was approached by Brigadier Bishop, the President of the Army club, and told that Army had received the go-ahead to form a team for the 1952 Olympics. He asked me if I would consider a transfer to the Army and be re-commissioned in the Infantry Corps.

"I finished up my wartime RCAF service as a Flying Officer. I was told that I would be a member of the proposed Olympic team. It took me all of about 10 seconds to say YES. About three weeks later I was on my way to Camp Borden, Ontario, for a Basic Officers' course as a Second Lieutenant.

"Just prior to the end of my course, I received a phone call from Brigadier Bishop telling me the Olympics plans had been cancelled because of the Korean conflict. I was posted to the Princess Patricia's Canadian Light Infantry and spent the next 14 months in Korea as a platoon commander.

"After Korea I was posted to 2 Canadian Guards in Petawawa as a Captain. I was posted to Headquarters, British Columbia, in 1956 and spent nine years there in various staff appointments.

"I was posted to Canadian Forces Training Command in 1965 and honorably discharged in 1967.

"I transferred to the Cadet Instructor list in 1970 and spent the next 16 years as a call-out instructor at Cadet camps.

"I spent 40 years of service in wartime and peacetime – in Regular Forces and Reserve Forces – and I would do it all again."

He is entitled to wear an even dozen campaign stars and decorations from World War Two and Korea.

He retired with the rank of Major to British Columbia where a job managing a curling rink awaited him. His two sons and three grandchildren live in Vancouver. Roy lives in Winfield.

"We are a close family and our favorite pastime is fly fishing in our mountain lake."

## HUBIE BROOKS
### MILITARY CROSS, MENTION IN DISPATCH, POLISH CROSS OF VALOUR, POLISH SILVER CROSS OF MERIT WITH SWORDS

Flight Lieutenant Hubie Brooks had an unbelievable war.

He was one of five Royal Canadian Air Force officers to be awarded a Military Cross. He was also Mentioned in Dispatches and decorated by the Polish Government-in-exile.

His real life war story is one that Hollywood scriptwriters salivate over. Had he been an American, there is no question that Tinseltown would have made a film of his incredible exploits.

Hubie Brooks enlisted in the RCAF on August 14, 1940, but he was not commissioned until 1944 when he was an escaped Prisoner of War, fighting with Polish partisans.

Hubie Brooks was a member of 419 (Moose) Squadron.

On April 8, 1942, he was the navigator and bomb aimer of a Wellington bomber assigned to attack Hamburg.

Prior to arriving at its target, the craft caught fire and had to be abandoned.

Brooks bailed out and landed near Oldenburg, just east of Bremen. Despite being badly injured, he buried his parachute and set out to avoid capture. But, his injuries were so serious he was forced to seek help and was handed over to a German garrison.

He was incarcerated in a prisoner of war camp from April 16, 1942, to May, 1943. During that year he made three escape attempts.

Brooks and a companion cut barbed wire on their barracks window and then cut through the double perimeter wire. The compound was illuminated by floodlights and patrolled by sentries. They traveled by night and subsisted on food they had saved from Red Cross parcels.

They were traveling towards Cracow and were recaptured when pro-Nazi Poles turned them in. Brooks was returned to the prison camp, interrogated and placed in solitary confinement for two weeks. Then, he was hospitalized because of badly blistered feet.

His second escape attempt was September 10, 1942. He escaped with five other prisoners from the top floor of a jail despite the fact there were armed guards on the ground floor. He walked to Lunenburg and successfully concealed himself on a train to Vienna where he was again captured.

While being transported to another PoW camp, he was badly beaten by a German soldier for trying to escape. He was locked in solitary confinement for 14 days.

He was sent to work in a sawmill at Toszek, Poland, and immediately began to plan a third escape. Somehow, his German captors got wind of his plans and Brooks was warned he would be shot if he attempted another escape.

Brooks improvised and came up with another escape plan. He made contact with friendly Poles outside the camp and they provided him with maps, false papers and civilian clothes.

On May 10, 1943, Brooks and a sergeant cut through window bars and made good their escape. They made their way northeast to Czestochowa where they joined up with Polish partisan fighters.

Brooks remained with the Polish guerilla fighters until Russians liberated him in January, 1945. The Polish Home Army promoted him to officer rank in the Partisan Unit of the Polish Home Army. The Polish Government-in-exile awarded him the Polish Cross of Valour on January 20, 1945, and the Polish Silver Cross of Merit with Swords on January 25, 1945.

The citation that accompanied his Polish medals reads partially: "...he took part in many ambushes and attacks on the Germans."

The Commander of the Polish Underground Army decorated him and the awards were confirmed by the Government-in-exile in London, England.

The medals created problems for the RCAF and Canada's Defence Department.

The communist government in Warsaw questioned the moral authority of the Commander of the Underground Army and the Polish Government-in-exile in London.

The RCAF and Defence Department chose the wisest course. They did not take sides. They did nothing. Hubie Brooks was not permitted to wear the medals he was awarded in January, 1945.

Finally, on October 15, 1947, Brooks was given permission to wear the Polish decorations and ribbons.

Hubie Brooks was born in Peace River, Alberta, on December 29, 1921, but moved to Montreal when he was a young boy. He played junior hockey there but his developmental years were stolen from him when, as an 18-year old, he joined the RCAF.

Hubie Brooks was not an especially gifted hockey player but his other assets made him a valuable public relations property for the RCAF and the Flyers' hockey team. He was a genuine war hero and he had a Military Cross and Polish gongs to prove it. He also spoke several languages.

"Sandy" Watson recalls that, at the time, External Affairs told him the communist bloc was spreading the rumor that the RCAF team was not really a military team but a group of professional hockey players.

"We felt that by including Hubie on the roster we could scotch that rumour. We could carry 17 players on our roster but Coach Frank Boucher could only dress 11 players. Hubie didn't play in the Olympics but he played in a lot of the exhibition games before and after.

"Hubie was invaluable to us. He put the communists' rumor to bed. He spoke several languages. He was familiar with Eastern Europe. He was known in the Eastern bloc as a war hero – one of their own – and he had the medals to prove it.

"Brooksie was a fifth rate hockey player – maybe sixth rate – but we couldn't have done it without him".

"The only time I ever even gently poached on Frank Boucher's turf was in Paris. I asked him: 'can you maybe use Hubie a little bit tonight. It would make me feel better'.

Frank said: 'OK'. Play stopped and Frank said 'Get out there, Hubie. You're on'. Hubie vaulted over the boards and tore off across the ice like a madman towards the Paris bench. He leveled a Paris player with a vicious body check and sent him right over the boards. The guy wasn't even a puck carrier and play was stopped. Brooksie just went over and hit him. The referee jerked his thumb in the air and Hubie was outta there – gone for the game – a game misconduct."

"In Czechoslovakia, Hubie was invaluable. We arrived in Prague a few days before the communists rolled in and took over. When the communists marched in, all hell broke loose. Officials we had been used to dealing with simply disappeared. Let me tell you, it was a very tense city and a very tense nation. None of us went for walks because there was a militiaman with a Sten gun or rifle with a bayonet on every street corner.

"Most of our travel through Czechoslovakia was by special trains the Czechs had laid on for us. At every stop we made sure we pushed Hubie off the train first. Of course, he would be in uniform wearing all his Polish gongs."

Hubie Brooks never lost his penchant for intrigue. One morning, at 2.00 a.m., "Sandy" Watson was awakened in his hotel room. Hubie Brooks was standing at the foot of his bed and he was wearing his RCAF uniform and greatcoat and there was an enormous bulge under the coat.

"Brooksie, it's 2.00 a.m. Where have you been? Are you crazy, walking around Prague? You could have been shot."

Hubie told "Sandy" he had just come from a meeting with the Czech Resistance.

"Sandy's" eyes bulged out.

"I just about had a heart attack. Are you nuts, Hubie, you can end up getting us all killed. Do you want to get us shot? From now on, you are not to leave this hotel unless you leave with the team and we are on our way to a planned reception or a game. Go to your room. Don't appear. I don't want to see out outside this hotel."

Brooks replied: "It's OK, Doc, I know the leader of the Resistance. He's a general. I fought with him with the partisans during the war."

The bulge under his greatcoat was a life size bust of Czech Foreign Secretary Jan Masaryk, an outspoken opponent of the communist regime, and documents the Czech Resistance wanted him to take back to Canada with him. The Czech Resistance leaders wanted to organize a meeting between Masaryk and the Flyers. They wanted the outside world to learn the true story of the communist occupation.

Two days later, Masaryk was dead. He fell or was thrown from a bathroom window in his apartment eight storeys up.

The bronze bust was smuggled out of the country in the Flyers' equipment box. It now sits on a table in "Sandy" Watson's Rockcliffe home's den.

After the Olympic Games hockey tournament ended Hubie Brooks married his Danish bride, Birthe Grontved, in a small chapel in St. Moritz. He had met her in Copenhagen while he was posted to a missing persons section. He wired her from Ottawa that he would be in St. Moritz for the Olympics. They agreed their wedding would take place the day following the hockey tournament.

Birthe Grontved was a petite 5' 2" Danish beauty. Ab Renaud describes her as "an Ingrid Bergman look-alike."

Group Captain Robert Cameron of Toronto and Winnipeg, Air Attache at the Canadian Embassy in Prague, gave the bride away. Barbara Ann Scott was Maid of Honor. "Sandy" Watson was Best Man. The newly weds exited the chapel through an archway of hockey sticks held up by Hubie's teammates. The Brooks settled down in Ottawa and Hubie became the overseer of the University of Ottawa's physical plant. He passed away in 1984.

## IRVING TAYLOR

Corporal Irving Taylor was a 28-year old, 175-pound right-winger. He was born in Ottawa August 13, 1919.

He was raised on farms in Chelsea, Quebec, and Carp, Ontario, and, like most young Canadian kids played his early hockey on ponds, lakes, rivers and outdoor rinks.

Irving Taylor was a promising young junior player in Ottawa and area and a member of Perth Blue Wings, winners of the Ottawa Citizen shield. He also played some hockey in the Toronto area with Toronto Goodyears.

He joined the Royal Canadian Air Force in 1938 and served in Supplies and Services in Trenton, Rockcliffe and Foymount until he retired in 1965.

When he was an Olympian in 1948 he was married with three children. In later years, his family grew to five boys and four girls and he brought them up on a Corporal's pay. When he retired he was a Flight Sergeant.

The Taylor home was at the corner of Elgin and Catherine Street – the present site of Ottawa's main Police Station.

He was one of the founding fathers of minor league hockey in the Ottawa area.

He was one of the original organizers of the Trenton Silver Stick Tournament.

One of his early neighbours and friends was Ottawa 67s' and New York Islanders' superstar Denis Potvin.

185

When he retired from the RCAF, he managed the township of Gloucester's indoor arena in Leitrim. A commemorative plaque honours his service. He also held a post-retirement job as an officer in the Ottawa Court House.

Old timers in the Court House and with the South Ottawa Canadians' hockey organization and the Minto Skating Club remember his unselfish contributions to amateur sport in Ottawa

Irving was a Day One Flyer and one of Coach Frank Boucher's final 17 picks.

He saw action in Flyers' first game against Sweden but was replaced by "Red" Gravelle for the final seven games.

Coach Boucher would never say why he replaced Irving in the line-up after Game One.

Was it because he partied too well and too late on the ocean voyage from New York to Southampton?

Was it because he tried to stick handle through the opposing team and wouldn't pass the puck to teammates?

Taylor favored an injured knee but later played well in the team's exhibition games in Great Britain and the Continent.

When Hockey Canada and the RCAF honoured the Flyers by raising a banner in the rafters of the RCAF Flyers Arena in Trenton, four of his family members were present.

Irving Taylor passed away in December of 1991 in his 73rd year.

## LOUIS LECOMPTE

Louis Lecompte said: "I never thought an old man would be on an Olympic winner."

Flight Sergeant Louis Lecompte was the oldest player on the 1948 Flyers' hockey team. A 33-year old defenceman, he had played most of his hockey in the Ottawa area.

He was six weeks older than Patsy Guzzo.

In 1936 and 1937, he played on Ottawa senior teams alongside Des Smith and Patsy Guzzo. They defeated Valleyfield in 1936 playoffs and, in 1937, swept past Montreal Royals 9-7 in a two-game, total goals series.

Buddy O'Connor, Pete Morin, Gerry Heffernan, Russ McConnell and Johnny Acheson played for the Royals.

Russ McConnell was a promising senior prospect who was killed when his armed yacht, "RACCOON", was torpedoed by a German U-boat in the St, Lawrence River near Montreal.

His body drifted ashore on Anticosti Island and was the only body recovered from a crew of 37 sailors.

Louis joined the RCAF in 1935 and was posted at Ottawa's Victoria Island when he was invited to join the Flyers.

He scored two goals and assisted on three others. One of his goals came against Poland and his second was the insurance marker when Canada defeated the United States 12-3.

He was a member of the RCAF's Photographic Unit and, after retiring from the RCAF, he moved to Kenya where he worked under contract for the Government of Kenya.

When Louis moved his family to take up his new assignment in Africa, one of the very first things he packed was his skates.

He was an avid golfer and the heart attack that felled him struck him in the clubhouse of the Nairobi golf course.

He passed away in Kenya on February 21, 1970. He was only 55.

His obituary was a terse, two-sentence item in a Nairobi newspaper: "SURVEY MAN DIES. A Canadian citizen working for the Survey of Kenya under the CIDA programme, Mr. Louis Lecompte, died in Nairobi on Saturday evening.

"An official of the Canadian High Commission said yesterday that a Requiem Mass will be said at Loreto Convent Chapel, Valley Road, Nairobi, at 9 a.m. tomorrow followed by funeral at Langata Cemetery."

His skates were buried with him.

Once a Flyer – always a Flyer.

"Sandy" Watson made sure that the families of '48 Flyers – living and dead- were not forgotten.

A little known aspect of Dr. "Sandy" Watson's professional career was that he was the "official" eye doctor to Montreal Canadiens' players.

On June 20, 1988, he wrote to 12-year old Louis Crawford Nancarrow, Louis Lecompte's grandson, and invited him to an NHL game in the Montreal Forum.

"You will sit 12 rows from the ice, just behind the Montreal Canadiens' penalty box."

## GEORGE McFAUL

There was no short list for the job of team trainer. RCAF Corporal George McFaul was everybody's unanimous choice.

Every amateur athlete in the Ottawa area was aware of the skills of George. He trained most of Ottawa's championship hockey and football teams.

George was one of the unsung heroes of the RCAF Flyers. He was equipment manager, medical orderly and trainer all rolled into one.

When the player's skates required sharpening during the Olympics, George took them by train to Davos – 30 miles away - to have the job done.

The players also did their own mending – sewing and patching. One night, Patsy Guzzo sewed up holes in his hockey socks, washed them and draped them over a lamp to dry. In the middle of the night, Andrew Laperriere got out of bed and turned the lamp on. Much later, Ted Hibberd rushed into the room. He had smelled smoke. Patsy's stockings were smoldering.

When players required sutures during a game or practice, George laid out Dr. "Sandy's" sterile kits and assisted during the stitching procedure.

Between periods of games during the Olympics, he served hot tea and lemons to the team. To show that chivalry still lived, he also served his brew to the opposing players.

The players called him "Black" George, The nickname arose because George dabbled a bit in the black market. Ladies' nylons, cigarettes, soap, razor blades and peanut butter were scarce in postwar Europe and George had come to Europe well equipped. Nylons, chocolate and cigarettes were more precious than a bar of gold in Europe.

He had so much trade goods that he broke up his stash and asked players to conceal the odd pair of nylons or carton of cigarettes in their luggage. Patsy Guzzo smuggled in several cartons of cigarettes and he didn't smoke.

Several of the players had their baggage inspected by Her Majesty's Customs and were assessed modest customs duties. Roy Forbes' bags were opened first and he said he was "nicked for $19.50 for cigarettes." George Mara had to pay $1.50 duty on nylons. The Customs inspection stopped when RCAF Air Vice Marshal McBurney, the Commanding Officer of RCAF Headquarters Overseas, stepped in and had a word with Her Majesty's Customs.

Ab Renaud recalls: "The girls came knocking on our hotel room doors asking for "Black George". They weren't familiar with the phrase 'black market'."

George remained in the RCAF until retirement and continued his work as a local trainer with hockey and football teams. He was also prominent in the Ottawa referees' association.

Over the years, the Flyers remained a family but George chose to remain outside the loop. He was the only Flyer who did not attend reunions or respond to invitations. Every Flyer from "Sandy" Watson on down is puzzled as to why he broke off relations. To a man they say he was "a great guy" and "one of the guys."

Now a widower and in his early 90s, he lives alone in the basement apartment of a building he owns in Ottawa South.

## MURRAY DOWEY

When he went to bed on the night of January 7, 1948, Murray Dowey had never heard of the Ottawa RCAF Flyers. He was unaware of their 7-0 humiliation in a game with McGill University or a 6-2 thumping by Bill Cowley's Ottawa Senior League Army team.

His telephone rang at 1.30 a.m. The voice on the other end introduced himself as Dr. "Sandy" Watson, Manager of Canada's Olympic hockey team.

"Dick Ball, Wally Halder and George Mara tell me that, next to "Turk" Broda, you are the best goaltender in Toronto. How would you like to join the RCAF Flyers and come to the Olympics in St. Moritz with us? We will be away from Canada for 80-90 days".

Murray was thrilled with the prospects of representing Canada but he wasn't sure he could get time off from his job with the Toronto Transit Commission.

"Sandy" Watson said: "Leave it with me. I will get back to you".

"Sandy's" next late night call was to Toronto Transit Commissioner Allan Lamport who later was elected Mayor of Toronto. "Sandy" awakened him at 2.30 a.m. and explained that the Olympic hockey team was in trouble. Their first string goaltender had respiratory problems and had failed the military medical. Lamport gave an immediate green light for Murray Dowey's paid leave of absence.

"Sandy" called Murray back and instructed him to be at Downsview Airport in three hours at 6.00 a.m. A special military flight would be waiting to fly

191

him to Ottawa. He was told to pack winter clothing for three months.

Murray's understanding with the T.T.C. was a two-month paid leave of absence.

Murray arrived at Downsview at the appointed hour and was advised all flights had been cancelled because of fog. It was his turn to awaken someone from his sleep. He phoned "Sandy" Watson collect and was told to board the morning train to Ottawa.

Dr. Watson recalls: "Around noon, this skinny, tousled 21-year old kid arrived in my office at RCAF Headquarters on Elgin Street. He looked like something that had just been dragged through a knothole. It was Murray.

"We walked him around, had him sworn in the RCAF and took him to Quartermaster's Stores to have him fitted out in an air force uniform and the rank of AC2. He looked even worse – like the army's 'Sadsack'."

Within hours, Murray was on board a CPR sleeper train to New York to board the "Queen Elizabeth". It was on the train that he met his new teammates for the very first time.

"Spalding sporting equipment gave us two sets of goaltenders' equipment. The pads were the best you could buy. So were the gloves, but I brought my own trapper and blocker gloves. My 'trapper' was more like a small first baseman's mitt.

"You have to bear in mind that this was 1948 and trappers and blockers were quite primitive. The only thing that set them apart from ordinary hockey gloves was that they might have extra wooden ribs stitched in the back of the gloves or taped on.

"A so-called "blocker" was nothing more than a regular hockey glove with a thick piece of felt attached."

The European teams were baffled by Murray Dowey's style of play.

Europe had never seen a goaltender like him before. He caught pucks with his trapper.

Fans arrived at games early to watch him grab off his teammates' shots in pre-game warm-ups with his quick glove.

Canadian Press reporter Jack Sullivan on Murray: "Dowey doesn't look like an athlete being pale-faced and slim but he has fine coordination and is not easily flustered."

In any surviving action photos of Murray in game situations, he is seen wearing a primitive cap that closely resembled a British cricketer's headgear. Murray says: "I never wore a cap before. I know I looked silly but I had to wear it to keep the sun out of my eyes".

Murray Dowey was, indeed, second only to "Turk" Broda in Toronto.

Murray attended a two weeks Toronto Maple Leafs camp in St. Catharines along with future stars Ted "Teeder" Kennedy, Gus Bodnar, Lorne Carr and "Bucko" MacDonald. The starting job was taken and the team only carried one goaltender in those days. If the regular goalie was injured, a replacement would be called up from the American Hockey League or one of their junior goalies would be sitting in a Gardens seat.

Coach "Hap" Day offered Murray a job as the Leafs' practice goaltender at $25 a week. Murray declined. His first love was fastball.

Harold Ballard was running the Junior Marlboros' hockey team and he offered Murray the starting goaltender's job - but no pay. Ballard told Murray he should consider the honour of playing for the Leafs' incubator as reward enough.

Murray disagreed. Other junior clubs were paying room and board, tuition and walking around money.

Junior hockey players playing for St. Mike's had their college tuition paid, their room and board paid and were given spending money.

When "Pinky" Lewis, the coach of the Stratford Kroehlers of the Junior OHA, heard that Murray had severed his relationship with the Leafs and Marlboros, he immediately offered him the starting goaltender's job and a job with the Kroehler Furniture Company.

Murray weighed the offer.

He didn't like the idea of long commutes to work, long bus rides to and from games, getting home at 7.00 a.m. and going to work at 8.00.

"I had a good job at the Toronto Transit Commission. I started there when I was 16 and my first job was as an office boy and my first take-home pay was $11.37 a week".

He spent 44 years with the T.T.C. and retired as a Supervisor in the Administration section.

Murray preferred to play senior hockey in the Toronto mercantile league and fastball in the Toronto area.

He played on the same strong Barker's Biscuits team as George Mara and Wally Halder: "I was doing all right. I was being paid $100 a game to play fastball."

When the Flyers returned to Canada with Gold Medals, Barker's Biscuits took out quarter-page ads in Toronto newspapers:
CONGRATULATIONS
TO CANADA'S
OLYMPIC HOCKEY CHAMPIONS

Below the caption were photos of Murray Dowey, Wally Halder and George Mara and below them:

ALL THREE ARE MEMBERS OF BARKER'S HOCKEY CLUB. TORONTO IS PROUD OF THESE PLAYERS WHO CONTRIBUTED SO MUCH IN BRINGING HONOUR AND WORLD RECOGNITION TO OUR CITY AND COUNTRY.

When Murray turned 18 he tried to enlist in the Royal Canadian Navy but was rejected on medical grounds: "I had bad asthma and hay fever and other respiratory problems. Then, lo and behold, I was drafted and spent the next two years in the army.

"I went through basic infantry training in Brantford and then I was posted to London. Then I transferred into the Royal Canadian Army Service Corps. By this time, the war in Europe was over."

Canadian Press reporter Jack Sullivan wrote of Canada's game with Italy: "It was a massacre and the Canadians were only half trying. "Murray Dowey spent the greater part of the game alone in the Canadian net." The Flyers won 21-1.

They were leading 19-0 in the third period when Murray suffered a momentary lapse in his concentration. At the eight-minute mark, Italian forward Enrico Menardi slapped at a loose puck behind the net.

Murray recalls: "Ordinarily, I'd have had a skate wedged against the post but this time I didn't get it over fast enough and the puck bounced in off my skate. Coach Boucher was just livid. He has hopping mad. I would have ended up with six shutouts instead of five if I had been more alert."

Shots on goal were not recorded during the Games. Only one instance of total shots has been found.

In Canada's 12-3 victory over the United States, Murray Dowey gave up three goals on 13 shots and American netminder "Goodie" Harding fanned on 12 of 18 shots, according to British United Press.

## ORVAL "RED' GRAVELLE

A broad smile passed over "Sandy" Watson's face when he remembered the late Orval "Red" Gravelle.

"Red was the 'baby' on the team. He was 19 and weighed 150 pounds of tiger meat when he began working out with the Flyers. He turned 20 just before we sailed for Europe."

Orval Gravelle was a "short, squat crowd-pleaser" from Aylmer, Quebec, just across the river from Ottawa.

He played Junior "B" with Aylmer Saints in the Ottawa and District League. His uncle, Leo ("The Gazelle") Gravelle played junior hockey and won a Memorial Cup with St. Mike's Majors.

Orval Gravelle played senior hockey with Montreal Royals, Buffalo Bisons and Ottawa Senators and 223 NHL games with Montreal Canadiens and Detroit Red Wings.

"Sandy" Watson remembers "Red" as a bellhop at the Chateau Laurier Hotel.

"Frank Boucher and I went calling on him and persuaded him to try out with the Flyers and, also, to join the RCAF. He joined up, earned a machinist's trade and stayed in the air force until he retired."

Orval 'Red' Gravelle was in the Flyers' lineup from Day One – from the 7-0 drubbing at the hands of McGill to Olympic Gold.

"Red" was a digger, a grinder. He scored three goals during the Olympics – two against Poland and one against Italy.

None of the goals was a big goal but his hard work on ice was a tonic and inspiration to his teammates.

His teammates called him "Carrot" or "Carrot-top" because of his flaming red brush-cut. European fans loved him; they called him "Rodenbroten" – little scrubbing brush.

"Sandy" Watson recalls: "he was a real star, short, squat, a crowd pleaser.

"In a game against Sweden, played before the King and the Royal Family, a Swedish player flattened him with a blind-side check after the whistle. "Red" was absolutely leveled. The Swedish player was all smiles and helped "Red" up.

"Red" didn't retaliate.

"Then, later in the game that same Swedish defenceman flattened "Red" again.

"It was clearly an illegal hit from the blind-side. "Red" rolled like tumbleweed all the way across the ice and came to rest up against the boards.

"He got up and skated towards the Swedish player. I said to my self: 'oh, oh, this is it. "Red" is going to sock him. He's going to take that Swede apart limb by limb'.

"But, he didn't. He just skated up the Swede, patted him on the back and said something like 'nice check'.

"It was the best PR of the tour. The crowd loved it.

"A top Swedish industrialist placed his limousine and chauffeur at "Red's" disposal and drove him all over Stockholm.

"Red" had his very first airplane flight in an RCAF Dakota during the tour of Europe. Coach Frank Boucher penned a few lines of doggerel for a Flyers' reunion 40 years later:

"Orval's complexion
Went from Red to green
As we headed for Prague
In that flying machine"

"Red's" stomach couldn't cope with the bumpy flight and he threw up, just missing his seatmate, Patsy Guzzo.

Ted Hibberd says: "Carrot was a favorite with everyone, played good hockey and won the eating championship".

When small town boy, Orval "Red" Gravelle returned home to be honored by the citizens of Aylmer, he said: "I wouldn't trade Aylmer for all the capitals of Europe".

He retired from the RCAF and lived in Trenton. One winter night in 1994 he was walking his dog and the dog slipped its leash.

He tried to catch the dog along double train tracks near his home and was killed when an oncoming locomotive hit him.

At his funeral, his coffin was closed but Murray Dowey remembers, "Carrot's skates were in the coffin with him."

## PATSY GUZZO

Patsy Guzzo was a 33-year old career NCO in the RCAF. Soaking wet, he may have weighed 150 pounds.

Patsy was reluctant to leave his family for three months because his wife, Mary, had just had a miscarriage.

"My mother-in-law encouraged me to go because it was the chance of a lifetime. She said she'd take care of Mary and I knew she would be in the most reliable hands. Also, I kept telling myself that this would be the culmination of all my efforts and a climax to my sporting career."

But, he was one of Ottawa's outstanding amateur athletes. He played hockey, softball and baseball.

He was among leading pitchers and batters on Eastern Ontario teams for a dozen years. Patsy was a double threat, pitching and hitting, from the time he was 15. He won 80 percent of his softball games over a 2,000-game career. His batting average was usually .400 or over. He played every position except catcher. On two occasions he hit three home runs in a single game.

In one season he pitched 61 softball games and lost only five. Pitching for a team from Bryson, Quebec, he won 47 games and lost only two.

His hockey teams went to the Allan Cup Eastern Canadian finals three times. In 1943, his RCAF hockey team was beaten out by the Ottawa Commandos who went on to win the Allan Cup. Patsy came in for some good-natured ribbing from his Flyers' teammates. It was no secret that most "amateur" athletes were slipped the odd dollar for gas or beer money.

Patsy was no exception. When Patsy's time came to sign the Olympic Oath, his teammates razzed him: "Patsy, if you sign that Oath swearing you are a pure amateur, the Olympic flame is going to flicker and go out".

Patsy turned down an offer to play professional hockey with St. Louis Flyers of the American Hockey League. Instead, he joined the RCAF.

Patsy Guzzo was a Day One Flyer. He survived every cut and was one of the final 11 players coaches Frank Boucher chose to dress.

When the Flyers were strengthened by the addition of five senior players from the Burghs, their first exhibition game was against a strong intermediate team from Belleville. Flyers won 8-4. Patsy scored two goals – the winning goal and the insurance goal 30 seconds apart. He also assisted on two other goals.

Murray Dowey describes Patsy as "quick." He was not a physical player and picked up six uncharacteristic penalties in the eight Olympic games. In the game against Great Britain he was penalized in each of the three periods.

He was Flyers' fifth highest point-getter in the Olympics with five goals and seven assists. He was singled out for his strong defensive play in the Olympics.

Not only did his opposing wingers not score; none managed a shot on goal in eight games.

In Flyers' first game against Sweden, the Swedes struck first. Klas Lindstrom put Sweden up 1-0 at 2.30 of the first period. Two minutes later, George Mara rapped in a pass from Patsy Guzzo to tie the game. Wally Halder banged in what proved to be the winning goal at 2.07 of the second period and Reg Schroeter put the game out of reach at 0:35 of the third period.

Patsy scored a hat trick in Flyers' 21-1 rout over Italy.

His big goal came in Flyers' last game – a game against Switzerland they had to win for a Gold Medal. Wally Halder scored what proved to be the winner at 4.33 of the first period. Patsy scored the key insurance goal that clinched the Olympic title on a pass from George Mara at 3.13 of the second period. Reg Schroeter put the game out of reach with a third period goal.

Patsy was nicknamed "The Bird" by the Swiss because of his speed and finesse. In Czechoslovakia, fans called him "The Dancer" because of his smooth skating and agility. French fans in Paris called him "The Angel". His teammates called him "Black Magic".

After the Olympic Games, Patsy briefly entertained an offer to coach Italy's national hockey team but he declined in order to continue his career in the RCAF.

Patsy Guzzo passed away in Ottawa January 19, 1993.

### PATSY GUZZO'S DIARY

Patsy left behind a 61-page, typed, single-spaced daily diary of the Flyers' 90 days in Europe. It is a sensitive love story of a father and family man, a unique hockey story, a travelogue and the wide-eyed jottings of a modest, gifted athlete – an innocent abroad.

A relative gave me a copy of the diary. One evening at an awards dinner, chatting with "Sandy"

Watson, Frank Boucher, Ab Renaud, Milt Schmidt and Reg Schroeter, I asked if any had ever read Patsy's diary. None was aware it existed.

So, I photocopied the rare slice of hockey history and mailed a copy to all surviving Flyers. Pete Leichnitz wrote back telling me "Patsy made me feel he was visiting with me."

. "Sandy" Watson told me: "I had no idea he had written such an interesting, entertaining and perceptive document. Patsy was one of the finest athletes I have ever met."

Andre Laperriere wrote: "Reading Patsy's memoirs was like being at a movie describing our past."

Patsy's accounts are so simply told but vivid that one can conjure up a phantasm of a wide-eyed, awe-struck groupie when he describes meeting honeymooning movie star, Paulette Goddard, and he new husband, Burgess Meridith, on board ship.

Patsy's diary underlines the abrupt transition from Canadian creature comforts to European hardscrabble living. England was still under wartime rationing conditions. Patsy wrote of their first London hotel in Queensgate: "William the Conqueror and his men slept there in 1066.

"It was so cold in the lobby the receptionist had on her fur coat, hat and woolen gloves when she registered us. There was no heat in most of the rooms. The odd room had a gas heater you could fire up if you had a shilling.

"I shall never forget my first English lunch – one slice of Kam, three small slices of tomatoes, a bit of lettuce and a small slice of beef – mostly fat."

"We traveled the cheapest rail class possible. The Czechs laid on our own special train for us. On rare occasions we traveled in RCAF Dakotas through storms and turbulent air. One Dakota was hit by lightning."

Patsy described the planes as "primitive."

He wrote that one flight "was so rough my seatmate, 'Red'

Gravelle threw up but missed me."

Patsy's innocently frank and candid diary records that one teammate (after the Olympic Games) who had been injured and would not play again "hasn't been sober since Brooksy's wedding.

Another entry was entirely Patsy's doing. He draped his hockey socks over a lampshade to dry. Andre Laperriere woke up in the middle of the night and turned the lamp on.

Everyone was awakened when Ted Hibberd rushed in the room saying he smelled smoke.
Patsy's socks were a write-off.


## PETE LEICHNITZ

At age 21, Pete Leichnitz was the youngest of Frank Boucher's "Black Aces" – one of five on the roster who did not get to dress for any of the eight Olympic games.

Pete was a victim of the numbers' game. Coach Boucher opted for veterans with senior hockey league experience. The only exceptions were Andre Laperriere, just turned 22, Murray Dowey and Ted Hibberd, both 21, and Orval "Red" Gravelle. Lou Lecompte and Patsy Guzzo, both 33, were the veterans on the team. The average age of Boucher's seven veteran players was 27.

Pete was one of five players from the Ottawa Burghs acquired to strengthen the Flyers. In his first game in a Flyers' uniform he scored two goals in an 8-4 exhibition win over a strong Belleville intermediate club.

He played well in pre-Olympics exhibition games but there just wasn't a starting spot for him unless there was an injury.

When news of the Flyers' Gold Medal victory reached Canada, Pete's father wired him: CONGRATULATIONS AND WHAT IF IT COST ME TEN BUCKS. SIGNED "PAW"

When he was 17 ½ he joined the RCAF Reserves and switched over to active duty when he was 18. Two of his brothers, Ed and Carl, now deceased, wound up as Group Captains in the RCAF. Another brother, Dilbert "Deb" was a Staff Sergeant in the Army.

Two of his brothers changed their surname to "Likeness" and told their father it was because it was easier to spell and easier to pronounce. Pete says: "that was bullshit. It was because German sounding surnames were not the flavor of the month then".

His brother, Ed, was a Spitfire fighter pilot whose assignment was strafing rail yards – "train busting". He was shot down in May, 1944, captured and spent a year in a German prisoner of war camp.

After the war was over, Pete returned to his federal government job with Revenue. He left Revenue in 1950 and spent the next 36 years with Canadian General Electric.

After he retired from CGE he lived in Brechin, Ontario, but moved to the warmer climate of Tillsonburg in 2003.

## REG SCHROETER

Reg Schroeter was always Mr. Dependable. He scored at least once in every game except the scoreless tie with the Czechs.

He finished third in team scoring with 12 goals and five assists.

Reg Schroeter scored two hat tricks – one against Austria and a second against Poland.

He scored the winning goal against Great Britain and three insurance goals. Two of his insurance goals were key ones.

He put the game against Sweden out of reach with an early third period goal. The Flyers won it 3-1.

In the final game of the tournament that decided the Gold medal, he salted a 3-0 win over Switzerland with the third goal midway through the third period.

Reg played all of his amateur hockey in Ottawa.

His career was interrupted by wartime service as a flight instructor in the RCAF.

Flying Officer Schroeter's return to civilian life after the war was also interrupted.

He was a high scoring forward with the Burghs when he was invited to re-enlist in the RCAF and become a Flyer.

After the Olympics he enjoyed successful careers in the federal public service with the Air Transport Board and the Department of Indian and Northern Affairs.

He had also refereed in the Ottawa area for 17 years.

Re Schroeter died from stomach cancer in September, 2002.

At his Memorial Service, eulogies were delivered by Flyers Ab Renaud and Andre Laperriere and his son, Tom.

Tom told the mourners present that his father loved to whistle: "if you wanted to find him, just cock an ear and you'd hear him whistle. He's the only man who could go around 18 holes on a golf course and whistle the entire score from a Broadway musical."

## ROSS KING

The late Ross King was born in Portage la Prairie February 6, 1919.

He was the goaltender for Portage la Prairie Terriers when they won the Memorial Cup against Oshawa Generals in 1942.

He also played senior hockey in the Maritimes with Truro Bearcats.

He was an RCAF corporal stationed in Whitehorse when he received the call to try out for the Flyers.

The starting goaltender's assignment was up for grabs but Ross King had the inside track.

Coach Boucher looked at nine or 10 other prospects. "Buck" Buchanan, Al Darlington, Doug Lyon, Joe Tunney, Bert Paxton and Trev Williams all had opportunities to strut their stuff.

An Ottawa newspaper reported that "new goalie Joe Tunney (from Newmarket, Ontario)" played goals in the Flyers' 7-0 loss to McGill in their very first exhibition game. He was the lone Flyer singled out for praise for "keeping the score down."

Chicago Black Hawks called Ross King up for two games in 1953-54 and he surrendered 18 goals for a 9.00 average.

University of Toronto net minder, Dick Ball, was recommended to coach Boucher.

Ball was the coach's first choice for starting goaltender.

His second choice as back up was Flight Lieutenant Bert Paxton from Calgary. Joe Tunney and Trev Williams were both cut.

Then, Paxton who had played senior hockey with Calgary Stampeders on the Allan Cup trail, advised Flyers' management he had been paid as a professional and could not honestly sign the amateur Olympic Oath.

Coach Boucher was hit with a double whammy 48 hours before the Flyers were scheduled to sail for England.

Starting goaltender Dick Ball failed the RCAF medical. A routine X-Ray turned up a spot on his lung.

The only goaltender left standing was Ross King until Murray Dowey was grabbed up from the Toronto Mercantile League.

Dowey played all eight Olympic games and most of the exhibition games.

He stayed with the Flyers for the agreed upon two months and returned to Canada in March.

Ross King played, without a back up, for the last month of the European tour.

Ab Renaud recalls that Ross King played outstanding hockey in the remaining exhibition games.

"He was a good goaltender."

He played 14 exhibition games. Flyers won 11, lost only two and tied one.

He had two shutouts.

In a 5-3 loss to Wembley All Stars before 10,000 fans – without Halder, Mara and Dowey - Ross took a puck in the mouth.

Team manager, Dr. "Sandy" Watson and trainer George McFaul ministered to his injury at the bench.

Canadian Press writer, Jack Sullivan, reported, "four stitches were necessary to close the wound. He continued to play after repairs and was one of the stars of the game."

After the game, Royal Air Force Marshall, Lord Tedder, went to the Flyers' dressing room to congratulate the players on their Olympic victory.

He stopped by Ross King and offered special words of praise for "his goaltending ability and his grit."

# WALLY HALDER

Wally Halder was, without question, the best amateur hockey player in all of Canada. He was equally at home on defence or on a forward line.

Jim McCaffrey, longtime manager of the Ottawa Senators of the Quebec Senior Hockey League, told the Flyers "Brains Trust" that "the best amateur hockey player in Canada right now is Wally Halder."

The coach/general manager of the New York Rangers, Frank Boucher, seconded the endorsement.

Twenty-six year old Wally Halder was an extremely gifted and versatile Toronto athlete.

He was team captain and leading scorer on the University of Toronto varsity hockey team.

Wally Halder was also the national senior doubles tennis champion and he was a swimming and diving instructor with the Ontario Athletic Commission.

Wally and George Mara were invited to the New York Rangers tryout camp in Winnipeg in 1946 and both players were offered no-trade, no-cut contracts by coach Frank Boucher. Neither wanted to play in New York so they both declined.

When his college hockey days ended he played in the strong Toronto Mercantile League with Barker's Biscuits.

After the Olympic Games he coached University of Toronto's Trinity College hockey team from 1949 to 1951.

His hockey career began with Toronto Young Rangers in the 1938-39 season. In 1942 he was playing in the senior Ontario Hockey Association.

In 1942 he and George Mara joined the Royal Canadian Navy as Probationary Sub-Lieutenants. Both served on corvettes and minesweepers as Lieutenants. Halder played hockey for navy teams between 1942 and 1945.

Goaltender Murray Dowey said that Halder and Mara had "pro shots" – hard-to-stop bullet drives only 11-12 inches off the ice. "Sandy" Watson says: "They had big shots – just like Charlie Conacher".

All of the Flyers had "heavy" wrist shots. The slapshot was still years down the road. Ab Renaud remembers seeing Alex Shibicky using a slap shot when Ottawa Commandos won the Allan Cup in 1943.

"Modern sportswriters credit Bernie "Boom Boom" Geoffrion with the introduction of the slapshot but Shibicky and Red Wings' Jimmy Orlando were light years ahead of him. Shibicky scored 110 goals with New York Rangers. I don't know if he scored any NHL goals using a slapshot."

Coach Frank Boucher describes Wally's style of play as "speedy and rough." Wally Halder was a fiercely competitive, hard-driving 185-pound athlete who could play center or defence.

Wally Halder paced the Flyers at St. Moritz with 21 goals in eight games. Between them, Halder and Mara scored 38 of the Flyers' 69 goals.

Halder scored the fastest goal in the Olympics – 10 seconds after the puck was dropped in a game against Italy. He had six goals against the United States, five against Poland and four against Austria. He scored four hat tricks.

In the game against Poland, Halder and Mara scored four seconds apart.

He was among the Flyers who were critical of European refereeing. As an example, he cited the instance when George Mara was knocked down and played the puck while he was sliding towards the net. Mara was penalized for not being on his skates when he played the puck.

Halder also dwelt on the "painful necessity of piling up huge scores. "We hated doing it. It runs against all Canadian ideals of sportsmanship. But, we had to do it to stay in this league against such competition as we got from the Czechs and Swiss."

Halder pursued careers in sales and marketing until his appointment as President of the Olympic Trust in 1970.

He held that position until his death in 1994.

### TED HIBBERD

Ted Hibberd is one of three living Flyers born in 1926. Murray Dowey and Pete Leichnitz are the two others. When Ted turned 18 on April 22, 1944, he joined the RCAF. He was posted to a Manning Depot at the CNE grounds in Toronto.

The war was winding down. He did his basic training and, since there were no openings in aircrew, he was discharged.

He returned home to Ottawa where a letter awaited him: it was his Army draft notice.

He was assigned to basic Infantry training at Camp Borden. He had an option: go to Missouri or Kentucky to train for the war in the Pacific or to Kingston for Signal Corps training. He reported to Kingston.

After VE Day he was posted to Peterborough. Personnel with civilian jobs were told to go home. A few months later, he received a letter advising him he had been honorably discharged.

Ted played junior hockey in Ottawa with St. Pat's, Hull Volants and Lower Town Canadiens.

His civilian job was with the Metropolitan Life Insurance Company in Ottawa.

He and his pal, Pete Leichnitz, were playing for the Burghs in the Ottawa senior league against Army, RCAF and Hull.

Ted was one of five Burghs invited to join the Flyers. He went to the Personnel Manager at Met Life to ask for a leave of absence.

"He gave me a hard time and said NO but I guess he was just doing his job".

Someone, Ted thinks it was Brooke Claxton, leaned on Met Life to release him and he was given the green light. Defence Minister Brooke Claxton had been a prominent Montreal corporate lawyer well connected with the business community.

He was also prominent in the Montreal Amateur Athletic Union. When he left federal politics in 1953, he became Vice President and General Manager of Met Life.

Ted scored three goals and assisted on four others in St. Moritz.

Ted is very high on Wally Halder and George Mara: "Mara was a great stickhandler. He could hang on to the puck forever if he wanted to.

"Halder was big, strong and aggressive like Frank Mahovlich. Patsy Guzzo was quick. Irving Taylor was a good stickhandler but not necessarily a good playmaker. He'd try to stickhandle past everybody.

Murray Dowey said Taylor 'wouldn't pass the puck' which probably explains why he played the first game against Sweden but was benched for the final seven in favor of Orval "Red" Gravelle."

Ted lives in retirement in Ottawa.

# POST OLYMPICS EXHIBITION GAMES

AROSA
FEBRUARY 11
RCAF FLYERS  18       AROSA  4

British United Press noted that the four goals scored by Arosa were more than any team managed to score against Murray Dowey in any game in the Olympic tournament. The United States scored three goals in their 12-3 loss to the Flyers and Murray Dowey gave up one goal to Sweden and a fluke goal to Italy. He had five shut-outs.

Flyers scored four goals in each of the first two periods and then poured on the coal with 10 goals in the third.

At the Hotel Schweiserhof in Arosa, Ottawa native Army Captain Arnie Charbonneau, Military Cross, threw a victory party to end all victory parties. Charbonneau was in Switzerland training with the Swiss Army ski team. There were a few walking wounded the next morning.

ZURICH
FEBRUARY 12
RCAF FLYERS  9        ZURICH  6

More than 5,000 fans cheered as Zurich held the Flyers to one goal in the first period. The score was tied 1-1 at the beginning of the second period. Flyers scored four times in each of the last two periods.

Wally Halder, George Mara and Patsy Guzzo all scored a pair of goals. Ab Renaud, Reg Schroeter and "Red" Gravelle scored once.

LAUSANNE
FEBRUARY 14
RCAF FLYERS   12          LAUSANNE  3

Wally Halder broke loose for four goals in a 12-3 romp over Lausanne before 10,000 fans. George Mara and Reg Schroeter both scored twice.


BERN
FEBRUARY 15
RCAF FLYERS   5          BERN  2

Ted Hibberd and Reg Schroeter led the way with pairs of goals as the Flyers defeated a Bern team 5-2 before 7,000 fans. Wally Halder added the single.

The Flyers boarded a train for Zurich to catch a 9.30 a.m. flight to Prague. At 10.50 their plane was airborne. At 12.30 it was forced to return to Zurich because of a severe snowstorm in Prague.

Finally, the flight left Zurich again at 3.00 p.m. and the team arrived in Prague at 5.30.

## CZECHO-SLOVAKIA

The Eastern European nation was then known as Czecho-Slovakia.

The Flyers arrived in Prague just days before Russian tanks and troops seized control.

Prague was dark and gloomy. Much of the city was still scarred from World War Two bombings.

The people were shabbily dressed. Staple foods were rationed and coupons were required for most simple purchases.

The Czechs were hockey crazy and would trade valuable Czech crystal for hockey tickets. Six hockey tickets might fetch three pieces of Bohemian crystal.

"Sandy" Watson recalls: "one morning we came down for breakfast and the man who had been the hotel maitre d' the day before was the new hotel manager. The former manager had been replaced because he was not a member of the Communist Party. All the hockey people we had met, we never saw again. All the people we had been dealing with, we never saw again".

There was no western press presence and, therefore, no summaries of the Flyers' six games.

Frank Boucher remembers that George Mara told him not to tour Czechoslovakia because "we were the world champions and why should we put our title on the line". He said the Czech national team would "tarnish our Gold by beating us on their home ice."

Frank bristles visibly when he recalls the advice. Fifty-five years on, he was still hostile towards George Mara and Wally Halder for leaving the team early and returning to Canada.

They left for Canada on February 27 to return to Toronto to help their team, Barker's Biscuits, in the Toronto Mercantile League playoffs. In fairness to Halder and Mara, their initial and only commitment was to play for the Flyers in the Olympics.

After the Olympic Games were over, George Mara and Wally Halder came to "Sandy" and informed him they were returning to Canada.

"They were the only civilians on the team and could do as they pleased. Patsy Guzzo wanted to go home too. He had a wife and small daughter and

I guess the pull of the home ties was strong. Frankly, he became a nuisance badgering me for his release. I told him he was our fifth highest scorer and we couldn't afford to lose him.

"Finally, Air Commodore Dave MacKell had to order him to stay.

"When Frank Boucher heard the news that his two star players were going home he became upset and mad – violently so.

"From then on, he was no friend of Halder and Mara. He felt that they had let the team down.

"I gave every player $200 for souvenirs in St. Moritz. I also took $200 myself and bought a beautiful clock and presented it to the Chief of the Air Staff when we got back to Ottawa."

The Olympics were over and professional Frank Boucher was now free to suit up for exhibition games with amateurs.

Other than practices and scrimmages he was long removed from competitive hockey. But, he quickly demonstrated he still had the moves and his deft scoring touch.

Frank wowed the crowds in Czecho-slovakia with his ability to flip a puck into the net. One of his prize possessions is a yellowed Prague newspaper with the headline:
FRANK BOUCHER = HALDER+MARA

It was especially prized because the team won without Halder and Mara and Frank was steamed up because they had gone home.

It was prized, too, because Czech sportswriters equated his skills to Halder and Mara combined. The Flyers played six games in Czechoslovakia, won five and tied one.

When they left Prague for Paris, the main newspaper carried a front-page tribute:

"AU REVOIR, FLYERS!

"YOU ARE STILL OUR HOCKEY MASTERS; YOU TAUGHT US BOTH HOCKEY AND SPORTSMANSHIP."

It wasn't all sweetness and light in Czechoslovakia. They played before 15,000 rabid fans on an outdoor, artificial ice surface in Bratislava. Ab Renaud was interfered with and retaliated with an elbow.

"I guess I rearranged a nose slightly and there was quite a lot of blood. I was sent off for two minutes for elbowing. The penalty box was located near center ice and it was right out in the open. I was pelted with snowballs. "Sandy" Watson told the Czechs if the rain of snowballs didn't stop he'd pull the team off the ice and call off the game. The snowballs stopped." The Czech player's nose was broken.

That night Ab Renaud paid for his sins. He shared a double hotel bed with Reg Schroeter. In the middle of the night, bed bugs forced him out of bed and he spent the remainder of the night sleeping in a chair. Reg Schroeter slept on – blissfully unaware of the unwelcome guests in his bed.

The Czechs pulled out all stops to welcome the Flyers. Special trains were placed at their disposal. Small town newspapers printed special extra editions. One special edition in Brno, birthplace of the Bren gun, headlined

CAN CANADA BE BEATEN?

The Mayor of one small town declared a civic holiday. A schoolteacher closed her school and brought the children to the train station for autographs.

Items such as chocolate bars, gum, sugar, soap, razor blades, cigarettes and nylons were only available on the black market.

Murray Dowey struck up a friendship with Czech goaltender, Bohumil Modry, and was invited to the Modry's home.

When he saw how little the Modrys had he contacted his wife back in Canada and had her send over a food package. It arrived on the RCAF's mail plane a few days later.

The Flyers were not above a little larceny. Many of them arrived in Great Britain with a supply of ladies' nylons, cigarettes, chocolate and peanut butter and carried on brisk black market transactions with bellhops and hotel porters. A carton of American cigarettes was like a gold brick. Nylons fetched $10 a pair – a king's ransom in 1948.

Trade in chocolate bars, gum, razor blades, soap, nylons and cigarettes was so lucrative players arranged with relatives back in Canada to re-stock their larders via RCAF mail flights.

The coach of the Czech national team was Mike Buchna who had played in Canada with Trail Smoke Eaters. Buchna was born in Czecho-Slovakia but became a Canadian citizen. His wife and children were not Canadian citizens.

During the Olympic tournament Buchna's strategy had been "kitty-bar-the-door" and he threw up a five-man defence. After the Games, his star player Vladislav Pabrodsky, dumped on Buchna. He claimed the Czechs would have won Gold if the players had been permitted to play their wide-open style.

Czech public opinion sided with Buchna.
Flyers opened their six-game Czech tour with a 9-3 win in Brno. They were so popular they stayed on an extra day and played an inter-squad game. The Blues defeated the Reds 4-3.

There was a method to "Sandy" Watson's madness. The team needed the inter-squad game box office receipts. They were singing for their suppers and needed the money.

From Brno, it was on to Bratislava by bus. The bus became stuck in snowdrifts and players were forced to get out and push several times. Flyers won 3-2 on the artificial ice surface.

The Czech Hockey Federation placed a special diesel train – "The Shooting Star" - at the disposal of the Flyers. It traveled 90 miles and hour and transported them to Ostrava. The train made an unscheduled stop at Bzenec. The Flyers' interpreter's sister lived there and he wanted her to meet the team.

Flyers won their game in Ostrava 2-1.

Budejovice was their next stop. Flyers won handily by a score of 7-2.

All along their route, the Flyers were heaped with gifts of silver and crystal. In Bodejovice they were presented with tastefully crafted metal cups. The cups were covered with a fire engine red glaze. Each player's cup was personally inscribed.

The Czechs left nothing to chance. They contacted their embassy in Ottawa to obtain the exact spelling of the Flyers' names. The embassy obviously sent over a newspaper clipping of a team photo with the names underneath.

As closely as the craftsman could manage, each cup bore a figure of a hockey player and the facial likenesses were almost photographic. Frank

Boucher's cup carries a figure of a hockey player who looks remarkably like him. Ab Renaud's cup is not as life-like.

When the cups were presented, there were two absent Flyers – . Front Row and Back Row.

Flyers ended their six game undefeated sweep of Czecho-Slovakia with a 3-3 tie against Bohemia. Frank Boucher, "Red" Gravelle and Reg Schroeter scored.

Flyers left Prague for Paris but many players left items of personal apparel behind for Czech friends. They were primarily pieces of heavy winter clothing, long underwear and heavy sweaters.

When they arrived at Prague airport they were in for a surprise. The communists would not allow the Czech airline plane to depart because the crew had no passports or visas. The players were then told that an Air France plane was on its way from Paris to transport them.

The newly installed Czech government refused permission for an RCAF Dakota from England to land. Finally, the mess was sorted out and they were allowed to fly to Paris – but not with "Sandy" Watson.

The Czech Hockey Federation had presented "Sandy" with a whisky decanter and glasses. The decanter had a map of Scotland etched on it. When "Sandy's" luggage was inspected, a 17-year old soldier saw the map with the etched names of Glasgow and Edinburgh highlighted.

""Sandy" laughs now but he wasn't laughing then. "When they saw the decanter with the map of Scotland, they took me for a spy. This 17-year old kid had a Sten gun hanging from his shoulder. They questioned me and held me for 14 hours. The team left by private plane without me. I was finally freed and joined the others in Paris. The Flyers all came out to meet me at Orly Airport.

"Let me tell you, I was terrified at Prague airport. I was scared to death".

The night "Sandy" arrived in Paris from Prague he " was besieged by reporters. There was no news out of Prague. I kept away from the politics and told the press how well we were treated by the Czechs".

The press was out in force because one of the Flyers' players "shot off his mouth and was quoted as saying there were no happy people in Prague and that there were soldiers on every street corner carrying Tommy Guns". The interview caused a minor international flap, which "Sandy" was able to skate around in Paris.

But, the Czechs did not buy his statement. "Sandy" narrowed the indiscreet comments down to three Flyers but he was never able to prove who made the remarks.


## BACK IN PARIS


The Flyers participated in a friendly three game tournament with three other teams from France, Scotland and Czecho-Slovakia.

Barbara Ann Scott and American Olympic figure skating champion, Dick Button, skated dazzling exhibitions. "Sandy" Watson recalls: "'Bunny' Ahearne was owed a sizeable amount of French francs by the Palais de Sport. He said to me: 'I don't want you to go on the ice until the manager comes up with the money he owes me'. I phoned the manager and he told me he would give me the money at the rink. I said: 'No, send it over to our hotel. We don't go to the rink unless we get the money first'.

"Shortly afterwards, a messenger arrived with a valise full of francs – bundles of French francs. I never saw so much money in my life."

Before 20,000 in a rink designed for 18,000, they thumped Czecho-slovakia 8-4.

Ab Renaud scored a hat trick, Pete Leichnitz and Frank Boucher both scored twice and Ted Hibberd scored once.

Their second game was against a team of Canadians playing for Scotland and Flyers lost 2-1. Ab Renaud scored the Flyers' only goal.

They played the game before 12,000 fans.

It was Murray Dowey's last game in a Flyers' uniform. He was returning to Canada the next day.

Ross King took over the goaltending duties and was in the nets when the Flyers defeated the Paris Racing Club 5-3.

Ross lost two teeth and required stitches when he was hit in the mouth by a puck.

He was back in the nets after bench-side repairs. Patsy Guzzo and Pete Leichnitz both scored a pair of goals and coach Boucher scored the fifth.

The Flyers won two and lost one in the tournament and were tied for first place. But, this time the numbers worked against them. They scored 14 goals but allowed eight.

Their final game in Paris ended at 1.00 a.m. Players were in bed by 2.30.

They were up early next morning for their noon flight to Amsterdam. The flight was late leaving. They took off at 3.15 and landed at Schipol at 5.30. There they were told they would be playing in The Hague, an hour away by bus.

Everybody now wanted a piece of the World and Olympic champions.

In Paris, the Flyers learned that the Canadian intercollegiate champions had challenged them to an exhibition game. The challenge was for April 10, two days after they were scheduled to be back in Ottawa. Coach Frank Boucher declined the invitation.

At the same time, a move was afoot back in Ottawa to award the Flyers a bye into the Allan Cup finals. Coach Boucher and manager "Sandy" Watson declined the honor.

## THE HAGUE

The Dutch Royal Family had issued an invitation for a Command Performance. They asked that the Flyers come to Holland and play an exhibition game. The Dutch government sent a plane for them for the one hour and forty-five minutes flight to Schipol in Amsterdam.

The team bus arrived in The Hague at 7.00 p.m. Dinner food service ended at 7.40. Game time before the Royal Family was 8.00.
Flyers loaned the Dutch team Roy Forbes, Andy Gilpin, Irving Taylor and Hubie Brooks and still won by a score of 9-1.

The next day a Dutch Airlines Dakota was laid on to fly the team to Stockholm.

The flight was scheduled to depart at 2.00 p.m. but did not leave the ground until 5.00 because of a low ceiling in Stockholm. The plane took off but was forced to make an instrument landing in Copenhagen.

They continued their journey to Stockholm by train. They took a ferry to Malmo, Sweden.

"Sandy" Watson recalls standing on a small deck of the ferry in a thick fog: "Horns were honking. I looked up and there was this huge liner almost on top of us. I thought it was the Queen Mary. It was a foot away. My God, I thought we'd had it"

## SWEDEN

The Flyers arrived in Stockholm at 9.00 a.m. after all night ferry and train rides. The players thought they had died and gone to Heaven. There was ham and eggs, pitchers of fresh milk, pickled herring, venison and some items they hadn't seen in weeks – Coca Cola and ice cream.

The players said it was the first time since leaving Canada that they saw milk placed on the tables by the jugful.

The Flyers played five games in Sweden and won four and tied one. Ross King had three shutouts In Aik, they defeated the Swedish national team 4-0. A Swedish team from Soertalje was sent packing by a score of 8-0. They defeated the Swedish national team again by a score of 3-2. Andy Gilpin and Reg Schroeter were both hit by high sticks and required stitches.

Flyers next defeated a strong Hammerby squad 3-0. Hammerby was the most popular club team in Sweden.

Also, while they were in Sweden they played an exhibition game against Dundee Tigers of the Scottish League before 5,000 fans. The final score was a 5-5 tie.

Flyers led 4-1 and 5-2 but the scrappy Dundee team fought back. Andy Gilpin scored twice and Pete Leichnitz, "Red" Gravelle and Ab Renaud scored once. John Evans from Edmonton and Norm Armstrong from Timmins both scored twice for Dundee and Johnny Rozzini from St. Catharines added a single goal.

## BACK IN GREAT BRITAIN
### ON THE WAY HOME

Flyers flew into London's Northolt Royal Air Force base. Their first game in London was a 5-3 loss to Wembley All-Stars before a crowd of 10,000. Frank Boucher, Patsy Guzzo and Frank Dunster scored the Flyers' goals.

Two nights later on March 20, the Flyers dumped Streatham 4-2. Roy Forbes scored twice and Frank Boucher and Ab Renaud rounded out the scoring. British United Press reported, "Frank Boucher was the niftiest player on the ice."

The Flyers were wined and dined in London by Canadian High Commissioner, Norman Robertson, and left the High Commission with a complimentary case of Duty Free Scotch whisky. Earlier, in Paris, Canadian Ambassador Georges P. Vanier received the world champions and they left the embassy with a case of Duty Free Seagram's.

The Flyers did not lack for strong drink because George Mara was not shy using his family connections to pry donations from his family's European suppliers.

Once the Flyers walked down the gangplank at Southampton they were under orders not to drink until after the Olympic Games were over. Manager "Sandy" Watson warned the team than any player who broke the rule would find himself on the next boat back home.

Back in London, the team boarded the crack British train, "Flying Scotsman", for the trip from London to Edinburgh and arrived there at 8.30 p.m., March 21.

The next evening a team of Scottish All-Stars went down to a 7-1 defeat in Perth, Scotland. Frank Boucher scored a hat trick and Reg Schroeter, Ab Renaud, Andre Laperriere and Andy Gilpin each scored once.

Johnny Sergenese from Humberstone, Ontario, scored the only goal for the Scottish All-Stars.

Two nights later the Flyers downed the Ayr, Scotland, Raiders by an 8-2 score. Ted Hibberd scored three goals, Irving Taylor had two and Frank Boucher, Andy Gilpin and Roy Forbes one each. Al Senior from Toronto scored both Ayr goals. The game was played before 7,000 fans.

On March 26, Flyers downed Dunfermline, Scotland, Vikings by a 4-1 score. Pete Leichnitz, Reg Schroeter, Patsy Guzzo and Roy Forbes scored Flyers' goals. Canadian Wilf Gorman scored Scotland's only goal.

March 28 – Fife, Scotland. It was time to come home. The Flyers were running out of spit. They had played five of their last games in six nights. They had traveled 15,000 miles through seven countries, played 42 games in 74 days, endured sub-standard lodging and meals and inconsistent travel arrangements. They scored 263 goals and had 105 scored against them.

They were beaten 7-6 by Fife, the last place team in the Scottish League. The Flyers led by a score of 4-0 before their legs gave out. "Red" Gravelle scored two goals for the Flyers.

226

Roy Hawkins from Kingston scored a natural hat trick for Fife. "Babe" Schultz from Collingwood was the Scottish net minder.

The Flyers' last game before they boarded the Queen Mary was against Falkirk Lions. Flyers won 8-3. Frank Boucher and Pete Leichnitz both notched two goals. Patsy Guzzo, Reg Schroeter, Roy Forbes and "Red" Gravelle all scored once.

Adam Bain from Toronto scored twice for Falkirk and Pat Casey from Prince Albert rounded out their scoring.

## HOMEWARD BOUND

The Flyers were in London preparing to board the Queen Mary for their trip back home.

Once again, they found themselves in the cold and drafty Crofton Hotel in Kensington.

The desk clerk was wearing her fur coat and woolen gloves.

They were given a reception at the Garden Clover Club where they saw television for the very first time.

"Bunny" Ahearne threw them a farewell party the night before they sailed.

"Sandy" Watson recalls: "Bunny" Ahearne threw a big party for us in London the night before we left for home.

"I thought so highly of him. It would have been so difficult for someone in Canada to organize the tour he organized and cope with currency restrictions.

"I asked Tommy Gorman if he thought he could have done what "Bunny" did and he just shook his head and said 'no way'.

"I have had three educations in my lifetime – a medical education, an education from T.P. Gorman and one from 'Bunny.'

"T.P. and 'Bunny' could run a country. They were that good."

George McFaul boarded the Queen Mary with one stick left. It was the much taped over goalie stick Murray Dowey used to rack up five shutouts.

Again, their liner encountered rough seas. The world hockey champion Captains of the Clouds were relegated to an ocean liner limping through a gale at nine knots.

The first night out a huge wave washed over the ship. Some of the players thought the Queen Mary had collided with another ship.

Four days later, the sea was calm again and the British liner plowed through the sea at 28 knots.

The Flyers learned on board from the ship's radio room that the Ottawa and District Hockey Association had passed a resolution that the Flyers be permitted to challenge for the Allan Cup.

The Queen Mary docked in New York at 4.30 p.m. – a day late.

Canadian Press' man in New York, Norman Altstedter, wrote that the Flyers were "rags to riches, hastily formed, scored victories in seven countries.

A young RCAF Public Relations Officer, Pilot Officer Bill Lee, was on the dock.

Air Commodore Dave MacKell, Bill Lee, and Ottawa newspaper reporters Jack Koffman and Bill Westwick boarded a tender and sailed out to board the Queen Mary before she dropped anchor.

The New York Canadian Club threw a glittering "welcome home dinner" for the team at the Waldorf Astoria hotel. Bandleader Percy Faith was among the diners.

Canadian Consul General in New York, Hugh D. Scully, noted the Flyers had played 42 games in 76 days, traveled 15,000 miles, played before 250,000 spectators and had a record of 31 wins, five losses and six ties.

Canadian Press chimed in with: "Flyers beat the Czechs twice without the services of Halder and Mara.

Earlier, Tommy Shields of the Ottawa Journal had written:

"A different story when they come home. What a rush there will be of back-slappers, stout supporters and all the rest. Everybody likes a winner."

The Flyers boarded a train for the last mile home. Players had been told their baggage would travel through to Ottawa in bond. Canadian Customs officers – four of them – came on board the train at Rouse's Point, New York, at the Canadian border.

Ab Renaud remembers, "They tore through our baggage like a dose of salts.

"They even stripped a wristwatch from my wrist. Then, somebody recalled there were news photographers on the train and invited them to film the search.

"Air Commodore Dave MacKell hit the roof and swore that the RCAF would never travel this route by train again."

"Hit with a double whammy, the Customs officers stopped rummaging through our bags, called off the search and beat a hasty retreat. That was some welcome home to Canada."

CFRA reporter Terry Kielty boarded the train at Montebello, Quebec, and rode into Ottawa with the world champions. He scurried from seat to seat taping interviews.

The Flyers arrived at Ottawa's downtown Union Station to a tumultuous welcome.

Interestingly, just a month earlier, almost 100,000 people had lined the streets when Barbara Ann Scott returned home with Gold.

The RCAF Central Band played "Captains of the Clouds". A fleet of Buick convertibles stood ready to transport them along the parade route. The Chateau Laurier Hotel's façade sported a huge cloth banner saluting the Flyers.

Silver Dakotas and a jet fighter streaked overhead.

The cars proceeded over Sapper's Bridge and down Elgin St. A reviewing stand had been built at the corner of Elgin Street and Laurier Avenue. Defence Minister Brooke Claxton, Air Vice Marshall A.L. Morfee, Ottawa Mayor Stan Lewis and George "Buck" Boucher took the salute.

"Sandy" Watson and Frank Boucher rode together in the same car. "Sandy" recalls: "Driving down Elgin Street I listened to CFRA on the car radio and they were carrying the taped interviews Terry Kielty did on the train."

The parade turned west off Elgin Street to Beaver Barracks where the team was honoured at lunch. Cabinet Ministers Brooke Claxton and Louis St. Laurent represented Prime Minister Mackenzie King. Air Vice Marshall Morfee represented Chief of the Air Staff, Wilf Curtis, who was out of the country.

By 3.00 p.m. the speeches and photo opportunities were over and the players were free to join their families.

Two nights later, at the Officers' Mess on Gloucester Street, the Flyers were honoured guests at a State Dinner. Three months earlier, they might have been asked to use the Trades' Entrance. Governor General Viscount Alexander of Tunis presented each player with a gold signet ring engraved WORLD CHAMPIONS.

The Governor General said: "The thing we must not forget is that Canada invented hockey, Canada gave the game to the world and that is why this Olympic championship takes on added significance. That is why I am pleased to see the World Hockey Cup brought back to this country where it belongs."

"Sandy" Watson presented Wilf Curtis with the World Cup.

The Canadian Amateur Hockey Association presented each player with a Parker pen and pencil set. Over the next few weeks the players were deluged with gifts from their neighborhood community associations, service clubs and their colleagues at work.

They were given silver rose bowls, gold watches, plaques, pen and pencil sets and expensive leather toiletry kits.

None of the gifts were ostentatious enough to draw heat from Avery Brundage's Olympic committee. Ottawa was not prepared to make the same mistake the City made when it presented Barbara Ann Scott with a canary yellow Buick convertible.

Before they broke camp, the Flyers played one last game together. An exhibition game had been arranged at the Ottawa Auditorium with an All-Star team from the NHL and the Quebec Senior Hockey League.

The All-Star team was composed of Buddy O'Connor, Phil Watson, Doug Harvey, Frankie Eddolls, Jimmy Peters, Howard Riopelle, Hal Dewey, Pete Morin, Gordie Bruce, Roy Giesebrecht,

Phil Maloney, Hughie Riopelle, Connie Brown and Doug Harvey.

The travel weary Flyers were no match for the All-Stars and lost 6-3.

Doug Harvey scored twice for the All-Stars and Phil Watson, Buddy O'Connor, Allan Kuntz and Phil Maloney each had a goal.

Hometown boys Ted Hibberd and Irving Taylor scored for the Flyers. Hibberd had two goals. It was an anti-climax for the world champions.


## RODNEY DANGERFIELDS

In the years that followed the Flyers were totally ignored by TV commentators during subsequent Olympics.

I suggested to International Olympic Committee member, Dick Pound, it was an oversight there were 17 Gold medals for players but no tangible recognition for "Sandy" Watson, Frank Boucher and George McFaul.

Dick relayed my observation to the Canadian Olympic Association in Toronto.

Their response was to present the trio with a "certificate and letter of appreciation" – the COA equivalent of memberships in a 4-H Club or the Book of the Month.

Sue Holloway stopped the "certificate" slight dead in its tracks. Hockey Canada President Bob Nicholson agreed to nominate the Flyers for induction into the Olympic Hall of Fame.

Everything seemed to be on track until the COA issued a Press Release announcing Edmonton Mercurys, 1952 Gold Medalists, were being inducted. Later, chatting with Gold Medal (1964) bobsledder,

Vic Emery, he was "flabbergasted. I thought Gold Medal Olympians were automatics. I've been in the Hall of Fame for 40 years. Doesn't 1948 come before 1952?"

## OSLO IN 1952

Edmonton Mercurys were selected to represent Canada at the Games in Oslo in 1952 but not without some controversy.

The sentimental favourite of many was a college team from St. Francis Xavier University in Antigonish, Nova Scotia. The Xaverians were Maritime collegiate and senior champions and Eastern quarter-finalists in Allan Cup play.

St. F.X. won the Maritime title and defeated Quebec winners, Dolbeau Castors, before being eliminated by Pembroke Lumber Kings. The Kings were a rugged, more experienced team with several reinstated professionals in their lineup.

Weekend Magazine sports editor Andy O'Brien wrote that St. F.X. was the only Simon-pure amateur senior team in Canada – so amateur that the players bought their own skates.

The Mercurys won Gold with a final record of seven wins and a tie. It took a Hail Mary goal with 20 seconds remaining in the game for Edmonton to defeat Sweden 3-2.

Edmonton racked up seven straight wins going into the final game with the United States. Despite out shooting the Americans 58-13, Canada could only manage a tie but it was good enough for a Gold medal.

The U.S. team was roundly criticized by the European press for rough play. Three U.S. players spent more time in the penalty box than any one of the other eight teams in the tournament.

The United States finished in second place and won Silver and Sweden defeated Czechoslovakia 5-3 to win Bronze.

It would be Canada's last Gold medal for 50 years. The Russians were coming.

## CORTINA IN 1956

The Russians exploded on the international hockey scene and won the Gold Medal with a perfect record. They outscored opponents 40-9.

Canada was represented by the Kitchener-Waterloo Flying Dutchmen who lost to the United States and Russia and had to settle for a Bronze medal. The United States captured Silver.

Canada had five of the tournament's top nine scorers. Jim Logan, Paul Knox, Gerry Theberge, Jack Mackenzie and George Scholes combined for 35 goals and 19 assists.

Surprisingly enough, goals for and against in the final five game round were remarkably close. Russia's record was 25-5, the United States' 26-12 and Canada 23-11.

The next quarter century was a lean period for Canada. The Kitchener-Waterloo Flying Dutchmen won Silver in Squaw Valley, California, in 1960.

Canada dropped to fourth position in Innsbruck in 1964, captured Bronze in Grenoble in 1968, finished sixth in Lake Placid in 1980, fourth in Sarajevo in 1984, fourth in Calgary in 1988, won Silver in Albertville in 1992 and Lillehammer in 1994 and finished fourth in Nagano in 1998.

# EPILOGUE

Fifty years after St. Moritz, in 1998, "Sandy" and Pat Watson and Reg and Shirley Schroeter were back in St. Moritz at the invitation of Canada Post.

The postal corporation was issuing a special stamp commemorating Team Canada's 1972 triumph in the Canada-USSR Summit and the Flyers' and Barbara Ann Scott's 1948 Gold Medal performances. The Flyers and Barbara Ann Scott were pictured on the First Day Cover's envelope.

"Sandy" Watson was Canada Post CEO, Andre Ouellette's eye doctor. Lester Pearson had recommended him.

"Sandy" recalls: "Andre said to me – 'we should have a stamp'. "He made it happen.

"We spent six days in St. Moritz as guests of Canada Post.

In the main square of St. Moritz there is a large cairn with a plaque listing the names of all the athletes who won medals.

"We were looking at the plaque when a tour bus pulled up. The tourists descended on the square en masse with cameras clicking. They asked us: 'do you know anybody on the plaques who won a Gold Medal?'

"I said, pointing to Reg: 'he won a Gold Medal in hockey here in 1948. He has his Gold Medal in his pocket'. Well, the cameras clicked into overtime. Kodak made a fortune, thanks to us, that day.

"Reg said: "we should come back again tomorrow and sell hamburgers'.

"We went to the Palace Hotel in St. Moritz – one of the great hotels for the jet set in Europe.

wasn't included in our budget in 1948. Paulette Goddard and her new husband, Burgess Meridith and Johnny Weismuller, the movie's Tarzan, were on the Queen Elizabeth with us when we came over in 1948 and they stayed there.

"The hotel owned one of the rinks we played on. Back in 1948, I said to no one in particular: 'I'd love to come back here and stay at this hotel'.

"So, I said to Reg and our wives: 'let's go in and see where the rink was and have pastry and coffee'.

"We told our waiter we had played hockey [down there] in the 1948 Olympics. Well, he told someone and the manager and his entire staff came by. They sat us at a table overlooking the rink."

Nearby, there is a plinth with a bronze plaque:
 ST MORITZ  OLYMPISCHE WINTERSPIELE.

The names of the 1948 RCAF Flyers are listed. Most of the names are mis-spelled and Irving Taylor's name is missing, even though he played one game in the eight-game series.
The names of Murray Dowey, Walter (Wally) Halder, Reginald (Reg) Schroeter, Patrick (Patsy) Guzzo, Albert (Ab) Renaud and Orval Gravelle are either correct or almost correct.
Louis Lecompte's name is mis-spelled – "John."
Ted Hibberd's name is mis-spelled – "Thomas."
Frank Dunster's name is mis-spelled – "Bernhard."
George Mara's name is mis-spelled – "Georges."
Andre Laperriere's name is mis-spelled – "Henri."

Ten Flyers'have passed on to their eternal rewards – Hubie Brooks, Frank Dunster, Patsy Guzzo, Reg Schroeter, Wally Halder, Ross King, Louis

Lecompte, Orval Gravelle, Irving Taylor and George Mara.

Coach Frank Boucher and "Sandy" Watson passed away in 2003.

There are seven living Flyers' skaters – Murray Dowey, Roy Forbes, Andy Gilpin, Ted Hibberd, Andre Laperriere, Pete Leichnitz, and Ab Renaud – and Trainer George McFaul.

George Mara is a Member of the Sports Hall of Fame as a Builder because of his service to the Olympic Trust.

"Sandy" Watson was inducted into the Order of Canada.

The 1948 RCAF Flyers' Gold Medal Hockey team is not in the Hockey Hall of Fame or the Sports Hall of Fame. None of the individual players has ever been inducted into the Hockey or Sports Halls of Fame.

When the World and Olympic Gold Medalists arrived back in Ottawa the first telegram "Sandy" Watson received was from Conn Smythe. He wanted the Flyers for an exhibition game at Maple Leaf Gardens.

"Sandy" ignored the telegram. Tit for tat!

Canada's armed forces voted the 1948 RCAF Flyers as their top athletes of the 20th Century – surpassing four-time Boston Marathon winner Gerard Cote and Olympic shooters Gilbert Boa and Gerry Ouellette.

Prophets are, indeed, without honour in their own country.

# INDEX

Manor House Publishing
www.manor-house.biz  905-648-2193